The Joys
of Complaining

Also by Jasper Griegson and published by Robson Books

The Complainer's Guide to Getting Even

The Joys
of Complaining

The Complainer's Guide
to Getting Even *More*

Jasper Griegson

Robson Books

To my Grandma,
who to my knowledge has
never complained about
anything at all in
90 years

First published in Great Britain in 1998 by Robson Books Ltd, Bolsover House, 5-6 Clipstone Street, London W1P 8LE

Cartoons © Neil Kerber

Designed by Harold King

British Library Cataloguing in Publication Data
A catalogue record for this title is available from the British Library

ISBN 1 86105 166 2

Typeset by FSH Print and Production Ltd., London
Printed in Great Britain by Creative, Print & Design, Wales

Contents

1
The Joy of Complaining

The British are no good at football. This sad state of affairs is now beyond dispute. We are destined to spend eternity trapped in a time warp facing nothing but endless re-runs of the 1966 World Cup Final. They think it's all over. It is.

If we are bad at football however we are even worse at one other activity. Complaining.

The British are very good at whinging but whinging is not the same as complaining. Whinging means moaning about something but not actually doing anything to resolve the problem. Complaining is a much more positive exercise but one which the inhabitants of this country are notoriously useless at doing. When disaster strikes at, for example, a restaurant, what the British prefer to do is mutter amongst themselves, saying that they're not bloody coming here again even if you paid them. They will stomp out dissatisfied but do nothing.

One theory for this wimpish behaviour is the weather. The British have spent far too long hiding under bus shelters, umbrellas and grey raincoats. Worse still, for long stretches during the winter months the British hibernate inside nests called suburban semi-detached houses where they huddle around a cathode ray and worship their gods,

Bruce Forsyth and Noel Edmonds. Although this behaviour should lead to cabin fever and a desire to head out into wide open spaces, it in fact results in profound introspection.

The other theory behind our diffidence is the War. The British are desperately proud of the Dunkirk spirit. By spending enormous amounts of time 'grinning and bearing it', the British came to associate expressions of dissatisfaction with sissiness. The manly response to adversity is the proverbial stiff upper lip. This is all very well if you are squatting in an air-raid shelter waiting for a doodlebug to drop on you but it really is not good enough if the problem is that a chocolate machine has swallowed your pound coin.

Whichever theory is correct, the net effect is that the British are shy and inhibited and therefore are not very good at expressing themselves. In fact, in many cases, they are afraid to do so especially when faced with the most feared enemy of all: authority.

The trick to complaining well is to stop behaving like a twitching rabbit and then go one step further – enjoy the act of complaining. I hope that by the time you have finished reading this book you will feel sufficiently bold and inspired to do precisely that. At the very least you will undoubtedly have a burning desire to take this book back to W.H. Smith and demand a refund.

21st April 1997

P.J. Norman Esq.
Director
Psion plc
Alexander House
85 Frampton Street
London NW8 8NQ

Dear Mr Norman

I wish to register a complaint.

I recently became the owner of the new Scrabble software for use in my Psion organiser. Unfortunately however, I have a problem with it and I would be grateful for your help.

For some time now I have been playing against one of the characters in the game called Anna Sutre. Such has become my obsession with beating Anna that I spend hours of my free time with her rather than my wife. My admiration for Anna's seven-letter words has reached the point where I take my Psion organiser everywhere I go, including my bed. For a number of reasons Anna has become the ideal companion since I stopped beating my wife (at Scrabble) – she is highly intelligent, she doesn't answer back, she runs on two relatively cheap Duracell batteries and she is always keen on sex (provided of course that the X is placed on a triple letter score). The truth is that there is nothing I like better now that a night on the tiles with Anna.

As you will see therefore the Scrabble software is so good that it has created a love triangle between me, my wife and a microchip. This is leading to an irretrievable breakdown in my marriage.

I would be grateful for your urgent intervention. Unless I hear from you shortly you may find that your company has been cited as the co-respondent in High Court divorce proceedings.

I look forward to hearing from you.

Yours sincerely

J. Grieg

Jasper Griegson

PSION UK PLC
1 Red Place
London W1Y 3RE

Tel: 0990 134224
Fax: 0990 561046

24 April 1997

Dear Mr Griegson,

Thank you for your letter of 21 April to Peter Norman, our Managing Director. I have passed on your most entertaining letter to our Marketing Department for their attention.

I would warn you that Anna Suture is currently engaged to Craig Reel, another on line scrabble player, who may feel a little upset with your intellectual, late night dalliances with Anna, and as he styles himself as unemployed he may have enough time to take issue with you over Anna. Caution is therefore of the utmost importance (and a very large score on the board)!

Regards

Simon Derry
Customer Services Manager
Psion UK Plc

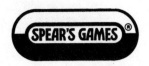

J.W. SPEAR & SONS PLC

Richard House, Enstone Road,
Enfield, Middlesex EN3 7TB. England.
Telephone : 0181-805 4848
Fax   : 0181-804 2426

2 May 1997

Dear Mr. Griegson

Thank you for your letter of 21 April addressed to Mr. Spear who is no longer
connected with the company. It has fallen to me to reply.

As far as I can see from your letter you are deriving much and varied satisfaction from
this product, which is produced by Psion under licence from Spears, and the only loser
in this 'affair' is your wife who is not, it appears, a customer of ours.

I think it unlikely that a company can be cited as co-respondent in a divorce case and
if you wish to pursue this matter I will be forced to employ the prominent barrister -
Mr. Joseph Tort, also present on the Psion game. As well as being a very able lawyer
he is the highest rated Scrabble player on the program, so I feel confident of success in
whichever field you wish to take Spears on.

I look forward to hearing from you. In passing, I note that your name very nearly
anagrams to RE: GROSS JAPING.

Kind regards

Philip Nelkon
Manager - Scrabble Clubs

Sir Stephen Waley-Cohen
Director
The Vaudeville Theatre
404 Strand
London
WC2R 0NH

9th February 1997

Dear Sir Stephen

Last night I took my wife out for a special treat. We went to
see Fascinating Aida at your theatre. The show was
excellent and we both thoroughly enjoyed ourselves.

Sadly, however, the evening was marred by a small but
significant detail which could, with a little bit of thought on
the part of your general manager, have easily been avoided.

During the interval my wife, having downed a couple of
G&Ts before the performance, needed to take a natural
break. The queue for the Ladies was dreadfully, and indeed
painfully, long. After finally making it to one of the two
cubicles, my wife had a difficulty to contend with.

What should she do with her coat?

For some bizarre reason, the door and walls were totally and
utterly devoid of a hook. My wife was thus forced to dump
her garment on the floor which was anything but clean.
This may be good news for Sketchley's but it is no way to
treat your loyal customers.

I would be grateful for your comments. In the meantime I
enclose a hook and two screws. If you would like to borrow
my screwdriver please let me know.

Best regards

J. Grig

Jasper Griegson

cc. Richard Hull (Theatre Manager)
Lee Beech (Master Carpenter)

Vaudeville Theatre

c/o Victoria Palace
Victoria Street
London SW1E 5EA
Tel: 0171 828 0600
Fax: 0171 828 6882

SWC/JET

12th February 1997

Dear Mr.Greigson,

Thank you for telling us. Very sorry. Thank you very much for the hook. Surprisingly we do have our own screwdrivers..... I think/hope!

I hope you will be able to use the enclosed complimentary ticket voucher for our next show at the Vaudeville. I cannot promise that the hooks will be up when you visit but we will certainly add them soon to our maintenance programme.

With kind regards.

Yours sincerely,

THEATRE TOILET

NOW WASH
YOUR COAT

Liam Strong Esq
Director
British Shoe Corporation Ltd
Sunningdale Road
Leicester
LE3 1UR

Our ref: f00t\loose

Dear Mr Strong

28th April 1997

Re: Shoddy Shoe Disaster

I have a complaint and this letter is written, for the metaphorical purpose of putting the boot in.

My darling wife is a sturdy old ox and is not prone to taking a tumble at the drop of a hat. Not prone that is unless one of the heels on her brand new shoes decides to unhinge itself at the top of the stairs. Poor old Bettina took a head-first Superman-style dive as a result of the enclosed item and nearly broke her neck.

Like your shoes, we are not well-heeled and cannot afford to waste fifty odd quid on shoddy goods from Dolcis in Oxford Street. I assume that the shoes which your company produces are designed to emulate your surname and for that reason I am most surprised at what I can only imagine is an extraordinary departure from your usual high standards.

I trust that your personal intervention in this unhappy saga will mean that someone at your end will do the biz. In the meantime my wife is left with only one functioning shoe and is hopping mad.

I look forward to hearing from you.

Yours sincerely

Jasper Griegson

BRITISH SHOE

Our Ref: JT/111548/Dolcis

8 May 1997

Dear Mr. Griegson,

We have now received the merchandise which you consider has proved unsatisfactory and the comments enclosed have been carefully noted.

On examination, we must fully agree that our usual high standard has not been maintained. Therefore, we are pleased to enclose our cheque for £ 54.99 being the purchase price and would like you to accept the enclosed voucher with our compliments.

We would apologise for any delay or inconvenience experienced on this occasion and we trust that future purchases will give the comfort and value which we strive to provide. Assuring you of our best attention at all times.

Yours sincerely,

Judith Tankard
Customer Liaison Officer
Tel. (0116) 2801431/2/3/4/6

11

20 February 1997

David Rigg Esq
Communications Director
The National Lottery
Tolpits Lane
Watford
Herts   WD1 8RN

Dear Mr Rigg

I wish to register a complaint.

Last night I was fortunate enough to win £1,329 on the National Lottery. I enclose a copy of my lottery ticket as evidence of this.

Unfortunately however £1,329 is simply not enough. My problem is that I am the victim of a rare tropical disease which has left me with a psychopathic lust for large quantities of chocolate. In the course of an average week I eat my own bodyweight in chocolate buttons. My winnings will barely tide me over to the end of next week.

Moreover, I rather fancied a luxury yacht, a small island in the West Indies, a private jet and my own chocolate factory. Those hopes have now been dashed.

My complaint is this. The number which I incorrectly chose was 12 as opposed to 36 which would have given me £3,500,000. If you could bend the rules a bit I would like to make retrospectively an amendment to my ticket. I have noted your second name very carefully and I assume that you can sort this kind of thing out.

Yours in jest

Jasper Griegson

CAMELOT

Operators of The National Lottery

25 February 1997

Dear Mr Griegson

Thank you very much for your letter of 20 February.

As you may imagine I receive quite a lot of letters from the public, many of which, I am sorry to say, bear a distinct paucity of humour. Not so in your case for which I thank you, as does my secretary.

As to your main request I have undertaken a careful reading of the game rules, the Player Code of Conduct and the Licence to Operate. Although your suggestion is not specifically covered in these, namely that we decide your number was actually 36 instead of 12, a layman's interpretation would seem to suggest it is a bit difficult to concur with your request. We could employ loads of expensive lawyers to seek further clarification but at the rates that they charge these days they would probably eat up most of the jackpot winnings anyway.

I think it is a case of better luck next time and if it is any comfort, I am not even allowed to play.

With kind regards.

David Rigg
Director of Communications

ipcmagazines

Michael Turner
The Managing Director
Fuller Smith & Turner plc
Griffin Brewery
Chiswick
London W4 2QB

Dear Sir

The George and Devonshire Pub at Hogarth Roundabout

I am Woman's Realm Magazine's Official Complainer and I write on
behalf of Mr and Mrs Worland

Their complaint is as follows:-

>   "The George and Devonshire's an excellent pub,
>   The beer is good and so's the grub,
>   But the one thing which the Worlands hate,
>   Is the decor's old and shabby state.
>
>   The surfaces show marks where beer's been spraying,
>   The carpets are worn and the seats are fraying,
>   The paper's yellowing on the wall,
>   The whole place needs an overhaul.
>
>   Though the bar's alright the rest is not,
>   It seems as though its been left to rot,
>   The fact that cosy this pub ain't,
>   Could be reversed with a lick of paint.
>
>   I hope that now you've heard my story,
>   You'll restore the place to its former glory"

I look forward to hearing from you.

Yours faithfully

J. Grig

Jasper Griegson

GRIFFIN INNS LTD.

DJM/14/PP

8th February 1995

Dear Mr. Griegson,

> I've had your note
> I like the rhyme
> So here's my note
> Please give us time
>
> The George & Devonshire
> Is right next door
> But just right now
> We're rather poor
>
> Next year we hope
> To make a start
> On work which will
> Make it look smart
>
> Then as a pub
> It will be fine
> I hope you also
> Like my rhyme

Yours sincerely,

D.J. Moseley,
Area Manager

2

Happily Miserable

To complain well it is a good idea to complain with a smile on your face. If you keep your sense of humour when all around you are losing theirs, you are certain to win. This is because even if your complaint doesn't result in a material victory you will have achieved success in two other ways.

Firstly, the mere act of writing a letter gets the complaint off your chest. Complaining is a cathartic exercise. It purges your soul by dispelling the evil spirits which, if left unchecked, will gnaw away at your mental well-being. By not complaining, you store up a guilt complex about what you should have done and you will be reminded at an opportune moment (if your spouse doesn't do it for you) that it really isn't good enough to sit on your backside doing nothing. By taking up the cudgels you take destiny into your own hands. Think of it as vigilantism by correspondence. The mere act of doing *something* about your problem will, I assure you, make you feel ten times better.

Secondly, by complaining in a light-hearted way to a cloth-eared old basket of a company chairman (whose capacity to laugh was probably removed long before his dodgy prostate gland), you gain the moral high ground come what may. If you're lucky, he (or she) may respond by allowing the scales to fall from his eyes like Scrooge at the end of *A Christmas Carol*. In that case, your gripe about a packet of iffy gingernut biscuits will meet with a profuse apology and a sackful of McVities finest. On the other hand, the miserable old duffer may decide that notwithstanding your cheerful approach to life's little mishaps, he is going to remain as happy as a Tottenham supporter in a red and white scarf. If that happens you can still content yourself with the fact that, at the very least, you tried and will live to fight another day. It is better to have complained and lost than never to have complained at all.

Unfortunately we live in an age when smiles come at a premium. I have a theory as to why it is that most people tend to concentrate on the rotten things in life – the skin on the semolina of existence as it were, rather than the creamy stuff below the surface. At some point in the middle of the 1950s, before the advent of European Monetary Union, scratch cards and speed cameras, most people were generally content with their lot in life. They spoke of their contentment in happy cockney voices and if, as occasionally happened, a crisis occurred, even one which threatened mankind, it was nothing that couldn't be sorted out by a nice cuppa tea and a couple of puffs on a filterless Woodbine. Suddenly in 1954, and apparently for no reason, people became disconcerted with this quaint world. Why? The answer lies in the classic B-movie *Invasion of the Bodysnatchers*. *Invasion of the Bodysnatchers* was not a movie at all. It was a documentary. The human race was replaced. The result was that the Earth became populated almost entirely by grim, swivel-eyed aliens incapable of laughing even when faced with the best episodes of *Fawlty Towers*.

The problem, paradoxically, is that miserable though we may be, we don't complain enough.

The following exchange of correspondence illustrates the point. Some time ago, the powers that be at IPC Magazines, the UK's dominant Women's magazine publisher, fostered trace-elements of a giggle. Their sense of humour often extended to employing my services. Sadly, this faint spark of humanity was snuffed out by the Dark Forces of Evil.

Allow me to explain.

I was *Woman's Realm* Magazine's Official Complainer. I decided to transport my cosmic capacity to complain into what for me was hitherto unchartered territory. Politics. My brief foray into the world of smoke-filled committee rooms and party political gossiping involved no more than a short note to the Personnel Manager at Conservative Party HQ at the time of the leadership battle between Mr Major and the Vulcan android Mr Redwood (see what I mean about aliens). Dr Brian Mahwinney, the Chairman of the Conservative Party, was less than pleased at my suggestion that I could do the job a damn sight better than either an extraterrestrial or a grey-haired wimp. He contacted his equal at IPC demanding my head on a silver salver. Rocked by a scandal of proportions equivalent to the notorious Inaccurate Knitting Pattern Affair of 1963, *Woman's Realm* duly obliged by ordering my immediate extermination. All future complainants seeking a slice of my wisdom may be well advised to direct their enquiry to the Executors of the Estate of Jasper Griegson c/o Hell. Hell, in case you haven't been there, is located near a junction between the A406 and the A41 and is called Brent Cross Shopping Centre.

Although I was disappointed that my career in politics had come to an abrupt end I have to say that I still foster a sneaking admiration for Dr Mahwinney's approach to complaining. No doubt having picked up a few tips from me, *he* went straight to the top and got a result. There could be no more fitting demise for me than to live by the sword of complaining and then die by it.

Realm

THE COMPLAINER

23 June 1995

Personnel Manager
Conservative & Unionist Central Office
32 Smith Square
London SW1P 3HH

Dear Sir or Madam

<u>**Vacancy**</u>

I am Realm Magazine's Official Complainer and I was deeply disappointed to learn that your party is currently behaving like a headless chicken. My readers and I, concerned that UK Plc is rudderless, feel that a strong, bold and strident leader is now needed. In my view, there is only one candidate for the job, namely me.

Although I have not been directly involved in politics, I was a school prefect at Oakthorpe Junior School in 1969-71. This position was sadly truncated following a bribery scandal; but let me say now that all allegations against me were completely unfounded.

Although I have never been a member of the Conservative party, a friend once joined me up for the National Front as a joke - please forgive me for that! My favourite colour is blue, although I have to confess that my allegiance is less towards your party and more towards eleven men in blue shorts who perform at White Hart Lane every Saturday afternoon.

I hope that in the light of the above you will give very serious consideration to appointing me as leader of the Conservative party. Unless I hear from you within two working days I will assume that the job is mine and I look forward to wallowing in the glory of your defeat in the next General Election.

Love and Stuff.

Yours sincerely

Jasper Griegson

No. 879
Friday
25 Aug. '95

£1

DR Brian Mawhinney's elevation to the chairmanship of the Tory party has resulted in total sense of humour failure at central office — and another body being added to the unemployment figures.

The body is Jasper Griegson's, dubbed Britain's best complainer, who for the past year has been hired by IPC magazines as the official complainer at *Woman's Realm*. While his letters have led to readers winning substantial compensation, he had not expected to have grounds for complaint himself.

Tongue firmly in cheek he wrote to the "personnel manager" at Smith Square complaining about the poor quality of candidates in the recent Tory leadership contest. Modestly he offered his own services, and wrote: "My readers and I, concerned that UK Plc is rudderless, feel that a strong, bold and strident leader is now needed. Although I have not been directly involved in politics, I was a school prefect at Oakthorpe Junior School in 1969-71."

Central office failed to see the joke and telephoned John Mellon, chairman of IPC magazines, demanding Griegson be sacked immediately. He was.

1 Virginia Street, London E1 9XP. Telephone: 071-782 4000. Telex: 262135.

Our ref: C.106

27th January 1994

THE COMPLAINER

M. Matthew Esq
Chief Executive
IPC Magazines Ltd
Kings Reach Tower
Stamford Street
London SE1 9LS

Dear Mr Matthews

I wish to register a complaint.

On page 31 of this week's "Woman" magazine an article has been published about me entitled "Meet Britain's Best Complainer".

Needless to say I am not at all happy with what has been published. My problem is not with the substance of the article but rather with the picture. In short, the picture is not of me nor does it even resemble me. The picture depicts a cretinous wimp who, by the look on his face would risk a brain haemorrhage if he were to have an original thought. If you look carefully at his pullover, you can see that it has been knitted by his overbearing mother. If you look carefully at the piece of paper in front of him you will see that he is putting the finishing touches to his suicide note.

In these circumstances I regard the article (together with the picture) as defamatory. Accordingly, unless I receive my body weight in chocolate raisins within five working days I will have no option but to take action which will give a whole new meaning to the words "drastic" and "sensational".

Yours sincerely

J. Griegson

Jasper Griegson

cc. David Durman, Editor of Woman Magazine

ipcmagazines

071-261 6452

Our ref: Griegson.February

Your ref: C.106

8 February 1994

Jasper Griegson
The Sun
1 Virginia Street
London
E1 9XP

Dear Jasper

Thank you for your fax dated January 27.

You don't frighten me. Sue! I'll happily pay up in chocolate raisins if we lose. If we win, I want payment in kind - gob stoppers.

Meanwhile, I would be grateful if you could send me details of your weight (verified by your company doctor) so I can warn Cadbury's.

Yours (wittily)

DAVID DURMAN
Editor

cc George Caveman

20 February 1997

Ms. Mandi Norwood
Editor
Cosmopolitan
The National Magazine Co Ltd
National Magazine House
72 Broadwick Street
London W1V 2BP

Dear Mandi

I wish to register a complaint of the most serious kind.

After parting company with £2.20 in order to acquire the pull-out to this month's Cosmopolitan entitled *Cosmopolitan's 100 Sexiest Men Alive*, I discovered with horror that I did not feature in part or at all. If Tony Blair was chosen, why not me? I too have got a hairy chest and an enormous personality. As for John Goodman - he could do with a few months on Rosemary Conley's hip and thigh diet. And Mark Lamarr - you must be joking! He needs a massive hormone injection and some spot welding at the very least. I, by contrast, am pretty close to perfect.

Being charitable, I can only imagine that your omission was a dreadful mistake and I therefore enclose a picture of myself for immediate publication. I have to say I look a bit awful in this particular photo, having just overdosed on a wheelbarrow full of chocolate buttons. I do however bear a striking resemblance to Ronnie Kray and if those are not excellent credentials, what are?

Yours gorgeously.

Jasper Griegson

COSMOPOLITAN
years at number 1

3 April 1997

NATIONAL MAGAZINE HOUSE · 72 BROADWICK STREET · LONDON W1V 2BP
TEL 0171 439 5000 · FAX 0171 439 5232
PUBLISHING DIRECTOR SIMON KIPPIN

Dear Mr Griegson

Thank you for your letter of 25 March in which you complain about the lack of a proper response from Cosmopolitan's editor Mandi Norwood to your letter of 20th February about the 100 sexiest men alive supplement.

Having not had the dubious pleasure of seeing your photograph I cannot really make a proper judgement as to why you were not included in our 'top 100'. To be honest, your description of yourself as having 'overdosed on a wheelbarrow full of chocolate buttons' is quite enough in itself to exclude you! It it's any consolation I too was devastated not to have been one of the chosen few and I'm the boss of the magazine! I held my stomach in for 3 whole weeks and contemplated expensive plastic surgery - all to no avail!

Perhaps I can placate you by promising to consider your application on our 30th anniversary by which time I hope either you or I will be past caring anyway.

Yours sincerely

Simon Kippin
<u>Publishing Director</u>

PS. I think you are unnecessarily rude about Mark Lamarr. At least he has talent!

Stuart Hampson Esq.
Chairman
John Lewis plc
171 Victoria Street
London SW1E 5NN

Dear Stuart

My wife Betty is a rough old bird.

Although she tries hard, she's no beaut. To be frank, a bit of spot-welding would not go amiss, if you catch my meaning.

Anyway, a few weeks ago, in a brave attempt to shore up her mug she bought the enclosed *Yves Saint Laurent Touche Eclat* from Trewins in Watford. Basically its a sort of crayon for covering up shadows, wrinkles and warts.

The problem is that this high class pencil has (a) gone mouldy and (b) stinks.

Please sort this out before my wife resorts to more drastic ways of making herself look better. Given that the alternatives could involve a book of spells, a cauldron, some frogs and a few tarantulas I would urge you to get your skates on.

Yours sincerely

J. Griey

Jasper Griegson

JOHN LEWIS PARTNERSHIP plc

171 Victoria Street London SW1E 5NN Telephone (0171) 828 1000

28 August 1997

SH/SJ

Dear Mr Griegson

I am writing to acknowledge your recent letter W1.tch.   We can find no immediate explanation for the pencil being in the condition you describe.   However, we have arranged for it to be replaced, and a new one is enclosed.

May I make the general observation, however, that complaints such as that which you raise are best dealt with in the shop where you make your purchase.   The Department Manager of Perfumery at Trewins could herself have replaced the pencil and would have been happy to do so.   Whilst I appreciate that some customers feel it is necessary to write to a Chairman to get action, it is the policy of our group to give full authority to our Partners in our shops to handle complaints such as yours

Yours sincerely

Stuart Hampson

11 September 1997

Mr Colin Short
Managing Director
United Biscuits UK Ltd
Church Road
West Drayon
Middlesex   UB7 7PR

Dear Mr Short

I wish to register a complaint of the most serious kind.

I commute every day between Euston and Harrow Wealdstone. The journey is nothing special: the scenery is drab and the train is often very overcrowded and hot. In the midst of this drudgery however there is a brief interlude which in some ways is extremely pleasant but in other ways is tortuous.

The torture is your fault.

At approximately 6.45pm my homeward bound train passes one of your biscuit factories. The buttery smell is so wonderful that at this point every day I immediately salivate like a Pavlovian dog. On a bad day I have been known to dribble like a geriatric and have even been caught in a doggy position with my head poking out of the window. The problem in short is that your company's assault on my olfactory senses comes at a time when there is no scope to indulge myself in one of your products: there is no buffet on the train and there is no biscuit shop at Euston.

In the circumstances there would seem to be to be only one solution. If you would arrange for the ovens to be switched off between say 6.40pm and 7.00pm the problem will not arise. I trust that a minor alteration to your baking schedule will not cause too much inconvenience.

I look forward to your earliest reply and a crumb of comfort.

Yours sincerely

Jasper Griegson

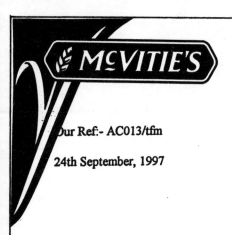

McVitie's (UK)
The Watermans Business Park,
The Causeway,
Staines,
Middlesex. TW18 3BA
Tel: 01784 447744
Fax: 01784 447711

Our Ref:- AC013/tfm

24th September, 1997

Dear Mr Griegson,

Thank you for your letter addressed to Colin Short, United Biscuits Chairman to which I have been asked to reply.

We were sorry to learn of the assault on your senses caused by us on your homeward journey, although it is illuminating to us at least, to learn of the effect of freshly baked biscuits originating from our factory! We can assure you that this isn't a clever ploy by us to subliminally mastermind the senses of commuter on your route.

We sadly regret that to remedy the effect of biscuit deprivation which you and who knows how many others undergo each working day could not be resolved in the manner in which you describe. For to do so for this 20 minute time period would deprive all too many biscuit eaters (our factory accountant suggests 389,054) of their daily fix - or is it dunk - of biscuits, and this as you know could leave a sufficient proportion of the population acting in such a manner to require a Biscuit Shortage Enquiry Unit to be set up.

Could I alternatively suggest that you could purchase our biscuits in "Snackpack" form which you could carry with you to work, and thus allow you to indulge in your favourite biscuit - homeward bound? You would of course be the envy of your fellow passengers! I am happy to send you some samples of the biscuit packs to which I refer under separate cover. Snackpacks are available for purchase from most small stores, newsagents and vending machines.

Thank you for taking the time and trouble to write to us.

Yours sincerely,

Andrew Cheale
CONSUMER SERVICES MANAGER

3

Abuse is No Use

The refuge of those who are unable to express themselves is abuse. Whether it be physical abuse or verbal abuse the net result is generally the same. Nothing. Not a sausage. Royaume-Uni nul points.

Abusive complaining doesn't work. I've tried it. On one occasion I failed to practice what I preach and reverted to offensive behaviour when complaining about a rotten meal which was foisted upon me by *Alitalia* on a flight from Pisa to London. It wasn't as though my complaint was trivial – I have complained in the past about planes banking too much on the port side or refusing to land in fog. No, this gripe concerned the *Alitalia* 'business class' cuisine which in my opinion tasted little better than pet food. I expressed my displeasure by sending one of the regulation airline sick bags to *Alitalia's* head office. Knowing that it is a criminal offence to send 'noxious things' via the Royal Mail I was careful enough not to send a full sick bag. Nevertheless, the would-be vomit receptacle was not well received and I did not obtain my customary gesture of goodwill. On reflection, I was probably lucky not to get a visit from the Sicilian brotherhood together with a gift-wrapped severed horse's head.

On another occasion I became the subject of abuse myself, but in truth I must confess to having quite enjoyed it. Following a television appearance on the much-maligned *This Morning* show my brilliance and charisma attracted the attention of a certain Mr Victor Lewis-Smith, the *Evening Standard's* TV critic. Not known for his charm or charity, Mr Lewis-Smith plainly thought that I was excellent material into which his metaphorical boot could be put. He described me as a 'Sad Herbert' whose time would be better spent writing not to large companies but to God, asking for a personality. I pondered for some time how best to respond – humorously of course. In the end, I worked out that whatever literary retaliation I might care

to launch upon the learned Mr Lewis-Smith, it would inevitably backfire. I decided therefore to let sleeping dogs lie. That was the case until a couple of months ago when I received a parcel from my brother who lives abroad. It was my birthday present. My brother takes an interest in African curiosities and had sent me a fully-operational, all-singing, all-dancing voodoo doll kit. It came equipped with a doll, some long, painful-looking pins and an instruction manual. If one day this year Mr Lewis-Smith's column fails to appear in the *Evening Standard* you will know why. He will have collapsed with an excruciating pain in his fundament.

Abusive complaining generally takes the form of a rabid rant. If executed at the Customer Services Desk it is often accompanied by the traditional banging of the fist on the desk. This method of venting one's spleen can best be described as utterly hopeless. It is Neanderthal and it is pointless but nevertheless frequently indulged in by the witless winger whose brawn far outstrips the capacity of his brain.

The other kind of abusive complainer will resort not to violence but to swearing in an attempt to bolster his minimal command of the English language. This is equally fruitless. It is quite wrong to assume that the lady behind the desk at Marks & Spencers is more likely to respond well in circumstances where the account of your grievance is embroidered by colourful references to copulation. A stream of invective will usually produce sweet fanny adams and no more. The cunning complainer on the other hand prefers a more civilised medium for the resolution of his disputes. The written word is always more potent than a punch on the nose.

The Managing Director
Alitalia Italian Airlines
Administrative Headquarters
205 Holland Park Avenue
London
W11

Dear Sir/Madam

RE: Flight Number AZ1260   24th June 1987

We enclose by way of service (you will not know what that means)
the following documents:-

1. Two "Club Class" boarding tickets for the above-mentioned
    flight from Pisa to London on 19th June 1987.

2. An Alitalia Sick bag.

As regular travellers between these two cities we would like to
draw your attention to the appalling swill currently being
dished out to the Club Class passengers on your aircraft. It is
quite dreadful to think that even at this very moment hundreds
of such passengers are being force-fed like battery-hens with
plastic trays full of the remarkable offal you apparently deem
fit for consumption.

Had it been practical, we would have sent you the gastronomic
garbage that was foisted upon us but to bring you up-to-date we
will describe the same for your benefit:-

1. Cold jellied pig with cabbage scratchings

2. More cold pig (apparently tinned) garnished with an olive

3. Yet more cold pig (a different colour)

4. Cold tinned vegetable

5. Cheese and broken biscuits

6. A soft roll that it looked like it had been baked in a
    plastic factory.

Had we been flying on the Bangladesh National Airline in economy
class, the equivalent "catering" might be described as
disgusting but the fact that this disgraceful food was served on
Alitalia was totally unacceptable.

We look to you for a substantial gesture of goodwill and would
like to have a full report on what steps you will be taking to
remedy this situation. Since we may well have to fly Alitalia
in the very near future we would be grateful for your earliest
reply.

Yours Indignantly

J. Grieg

Jasper Griegson

/Alitalia ITALY'S WORLD AIRLINE

| London | Your ref. | Our ref. UP14c/341 |

29th June, 1987.

Dear Sirs,

    I am returning herewith your letter dated 24th June 1987, which I find unduly impolite and offensive. We at Alitalia are not used to dealing with this kind of correspondence.

    If you would like to present a formal complaint, we shall be happy to deal with it.

Yours faithfully,
A L I T A L I A
Linee Aeree Italiane S.p.A.

P. Sani
General Manager for U.K. & Ireland

Enc/
PS/dfg

Patty
Espresso
Television Centre
Southampton
SO14 OPZ

Dear Patty

Our ref: Free chocolate

<u>Re: The Mother of All Chat Shows</u>

16th May 1997

I wish to register a number of complaints about my interview with you on *Espresso* which was broadcast last Tuesday.

- You called me "sad" on three occasions. The only reason you abstained from referring to me as a sad bastard was that *Espresso* purports to be a family show. I am not sad. I am very happy ☺

- I was led to believe that our chat would be a luvvy duvvy coffee morning-type chin wag. Instead, you subjected me to a gestapo-style grilling after which my confidence was in tatters. Have you ever thought of working for the intelligence services? .

- Towards the end of the interrogation you switched from hatred to lust and obviously decided that you wanted not just my intellect but my body. The comradely nudge which you gave me when I left was extremely telling. No wonder they call you Patty. I only turned up for the fee - I have no desire to become caught up in a sordid love triangle. Please restrain yourself in future.

If you send me a large packet of chocolate buttons I'll let you off.

Best regards

Yours sincerely

J. Grig

<u>Jasper Griegson</u>

27th February 1997

Sir Richard Greenbury Esq
Marks & Spencer plc
Michael House
Baker Street
London W1A 1DN

Dear Sir Richard

I write on behalf of a good friend of mine Mr Gerry Berkley who visited your Pantheon store in Oxford Street on Monday 24th February at approximately 1-20pm.

Gerry popped in to buy one of your excellent ploughman's sandwiches. Instead of being given the snack of his choice he was handed, in somewhat stark contrast, the smack of his life.

Allow me to explain.

As Gerry was leaving by the back stairs into Great Malborough Street he was presented with the least desirable form of lunch-time appetizer - a knuckle sandwich - or something pretty close to it. Apparently, one of your more zoologically wayward security guards unwittingly wacked Gerry in what can best be described as the penalty area. Gerry stumbled down the stairs and was badly shaken. The thrusting blond-haired zealot seemed to be in hot pursuit of a shoplifter. Let's hope he caught him! Gerry however was unamused having only a few days earlier suffered the trauma of a hernia operation. He hardly needed a midday thumping from a passionate primate.

When confronted by Gerry the security guard grunted a hostile and begrudging apology. Gerry was somewhat dazed by the experience and went to recuperate in the company of Jo Farmer the Floor Manager. She was sympathetic and explained that the employee in question was new to the job and was prone to "getting carried away". It would seem that a couple of tranquillisers and a bromide injection would not go amiss! In fairness Jo Farmer was very polite and offered the bruised Gerry appropriate first aid.

I can only imagine that you will agree that this incident was an extraordinary departure from your usual high standards of customer care. I am sure that bashing shoppers in not an M & S corporate objective. On the contrary, I trust that in the circumstances you will provide Gerry with a substantive and meaningful gesture of goodwill.

I look forward to hearing from you.

Yours sincerely

Jasper Griegson

MARKS & SPENCER

19 March 1997

Our Ref: GM1/1543949/006/FG

Dear Mr Griegson

Thank you for your letter of 16th March.

As already stated, the security guard in question is not a Marks & Spencer employee. I was also saddened that Mr Berkley feels he was assaulted. It must be made quite clear that it was certainly not an assault, but a genuine accident while the security guard was in pursuit of a shoplifter.

However, we do wish to make amends to Mr Berkley although we do not feel liable in any way. We note that, thankfully, Mr Berkley only suffered very minor injuries and he felt no need to seek medical treatment. In view of this we are prepared to offer Mr Berkley £200.00 as a gesture of our goodwill. This gesture will be made on the form of gift vouchers.

I look forward to hearing from you.

Yours sincerely

GREG MARSHALL
Corporate Affairs
0171-268-6566

SHOPLIFTERS WILL BE PROSECUTED.
NORMAL PEOPLE WILL BE PUNCHED.

THE COMPLAINER

25th August 1997

P.C. Sherlock Esq
Chairman
Bass Leisure Entertainments Limited
New Castle House
Castle Boulevard
Nottingham
NG7 1FT

Dear Mr Sherlock

The Hollywood Bowl in Watford,
Seemed an excellent choice to me,
For a game of ten pin skittles,
And a spot of afternoon tea.

My family went there yesterday,
I wonder now why we did,
An hour's worth of anguish,
Is what we got for our thirty quid.

The balls got stuck, the skittles too,
My young ones started wailing,
The scoring board and everything else,
Seemed bound to keep of failing.

We couldn't have guessed,
That our choice of lane,
Could cause such torment,
Angst and pain.

Our Sunday was spoiled,
We couldn't be fussed,
So we left the place,
In deep disgust.

I have no doubt,
That you will see,
The true extent,
Of our misery.

Please let me know,
How you intend,
To cheer us up,
And make amends.

I've said my bit,
I've described the crime,
So now I think,
I'll end this rhyme.

Yours sincerely

J. Grig

Jasper Griegson

Bass Leisure Entertainments Limited

New Castle House   Castle Boulevard   Nottingham NG7 1FT
Tel: 0115 924 0333   Fax: 0115 924 0657

15th September 1997

Dear Mr Griegson

We thank you for your letter in verse
Your visit it seems could not have been worse.
Bowling at Watford should have been fun,
Our facilities, we feel, are second to none.
We're sorry the "gremlins" got into your lane,
An experience we hope won't happen again.
We're really sorry this happened to you,
The staff at the Bowl are feeling quite blue
That the problems you had did not get put right,
It obviously wasn't "alright on the night!".
So to tempt you back and to make amends,
Please find enclosed vouchers for your family and friends.
We hope you come back and have a good time,
And on that note, I'll finish my rhyme.

Yours sincerely

R. M. Cave
Managing Director

Encs

17th October 1997

Charles Belcher Esq
Managing Director
Silverlink Train Services Limited
Melton House
65-67 Clarendon Road
Watford

Dear Mr Belcher

Re: The Lack of a Bench on Platform 6 at Harrow and Wealdstone Station

How do you make your way to work in the morning? I suspect that your trip is
not too bad. I have visions of you driving a 'P' registration Jaguar along quiet
leafy lanes for twenty minutes or so. On your arrival at your office there is
doubtless a reserved parking space and a friendly receptionist waiting to greet
you.

For my fellow commuters and I the journey into London from the suburbs can be
less pleasant. I catch the 08:52 North London Railways train from Harrow and
Wealdstone into Euston.

Although the trains are clean and reliable there is one fundamental problem
which causes me unnecessary grief. You would improve my daily life (and that
of many others) if you would take some action. The issue is this. Most of the
commuters at Harrow and Wealdstone wait on platform 6 for a spot at the back
end of the train. The reason for this is that the train (which has come from
Milton Keynes) is usually pretty full and the last remaining seats are only
available in the last carriage. At this end of platform 6 however there is no
bench. Nothing. Not a sausage.

I would be most grateful if you would spare a few quid and shell out for some
kind of seating. I really do need to park my bum somewhere, particularly on
those occasions when there is a delay.

My four year old daughter, Zoe, who sympathises with me no end has depicted
the true extent of my misery in the attached artistic masterpiece.

I look forward to hearing from you as a matter of urgency.

Yours sincerely

J. Griegson

Jasper Griegson

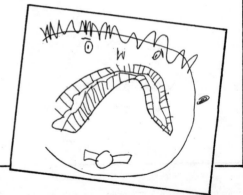

Melton House, 65-67 Clarendon Road, Watford, Hertfordshire WD1 1DP

silverlink
train services

Date: 24 October 1997
Our Ref: 192515/TC

Telephone 01923 207258
Facsimile 01923 207023

without prejudice

Dear Mr Griegson,

Thank you for your letter of 17 October 1997 and the picture from Zoe. I am sorry to shatter your illusions regarding my journey to work - no Jaguar but a four carriage Silverlink train!

I am pleased to advise you that we are in the position to accede to your request and expect to be in the position to supply you with a seat by the end of next week. We were toying with the idea of asking you to unveil it.... but maybe not! When its installed, Zoe can draw us another picture of you looking happy.

During the New Year we expect to be starting work at Harrow & Wealdstone station to spruce it up and remove some of the vandalised and redundant buildings. This will leave you with a more pleasant outlook to contemplate whist awaiting your train.

Yours sincerely,

Charles Belcher
Managing Director

Your ref:192515/TC
Our ref:N0.B.E.nch

7th December 1997

Charles Belcher Esq
Silverlink Train Services
Melton House
65-67 Clarendon Road
Watford
Herts WD1 1DP

Dear Mr Belcher

In your letter to me of 24 October you very kindly promised to accede to my
simple request by the end of the following week. I attach a document which sets
out my latest thoughts on the subject.

I look forward to hearing from you.

Yours sincerely

Jasper Griegson

Melton House, 65-67 Clarendon Road, Watford, Hertfordshire WD1 1DP

silverlink
train services

Tel:- 01923 207788
Fax:- 01923 207069

11 December 1997

Dear Mr Gregson

On receipt of your first letter, I arranged for a bench to be installed at Harrow & Wealdstone but I'm wondering whether it's on the wrong platform!

Could you telephone Matt Conroy in Silverlink Estates Department on 01923 207008. Matt knows all about your request and would be happy to arrange for a bench to be placed wherever you would like it.

I am sorry if there has been some confusion over this. However, if you speak to Matt, he'll be happy to oblige.

Yours sincerely

Anne Arnott

Anne Arnott
PA to Charles Belcher

25th December 1997

Charles Belcher Esq
Silverlink Train Services
Melton House
65-67 Clarendon Road
Watford
Herts WD1 1DP

Your ref:192515/TC
Our ref:N0.B.E.nch

Dear Mr Belcher

Thank you for the Christmas card but more importantly, thank you very much indeed for the **three** glowing fluorescent green benches. Are they radioactive?

As promised, I enclose a picture of me looking happy - as drawn by my youngest daughter, Zoë.

Thank you again for your help and good humour.

Yours sincerely

J. Griey

Jasper Griegson

Genuine complaint

AS A busy customer relations officer for a large manufacturer, I'm afraid 'Mr Greigson' — who boasts of being Britain's best complainer — is a far from lone crusader. We are constantly dealing with people who 'try it on' in this way and it saddens me that people like him can be so successful in their endeavours.

The world is full of professional complainers, and the more companies give in to these lunatics, the more the genuine customer will pay, as the cost of dealing with them finds its way into retail prices.

By all means stand up for your consumer rights, but 'walking around the house at night wondering what to complain about' is not on.

IAN SUTCLIFFE,
Guildford, Surrey.

I wish to register a most serious complaint: the Daily Mail article about myself, Britain's most famous complainer, was totally unsatisfactory. The failing was threefold:
1. The article was entirely accurate.
2. The photographer who took my picture was charming.
3. I have nothing to complain about.

To prevent me from starting defamation proceedings without further notice, please arrange for the customary compensation to be dispatched to my home forthwith. Two large bars of chocolate normally suffice.

JASPER GRIEGSON
Middlesex

Private and Confidential

30th December 1997

David Sainsbury
Chairman & Chief Executive
J Sainsbury plc
Stamford House
Stamford Street
London SE1 9LL

Dear David

Yours sincerely

J. Grieg

Jasper Griegson

SAINSBURY'S

Customer Relations

22 January 1998

Dear Mr Griegson

Thank you for your further letter to David Sainsbury. He has again asked me to reply and I welcome the opportunity to do so.

We were of course very concerned to learn that you found a hair in your purchase of our Pithivier pie. Clearly this lapse in quality control is unacceptable. Our Buyer is taking the details up urgently with our supplier.

Please accept our apologies for this. To make some amends, I should like you to have the enclosed voucher which you can redeem in any of our stores.

Thank you again for making us aware of this and for shopping with us.

Yours sincerely

Terry Wells
Customer Services Director

Enc. £15.00 voucher

47

<u>Private and Confidential</u>

David Sainsbury
Chairman & Chief Executive
J Sainsbury plc
Stamford House
Stamford Street
London SE1 9LL

Dear David

How are you? We seem to have lost touch recently but the enclosure to this letter will doubtless rekindle our relationship.

As you can see the can of Saisburys own brand cola exhibited hereto does not represent good value for money. Since it is entirely devoid of liquid it would seem that I have purchased nothing but fresh air.

I appreciate that if used as part of a calorie-controlled diet fresh air might enable me to develop stunning good looks and an hour-glass figure. The truth is however that my wife couldn't care less if I look like George Clooney or not - she lusts after my personality and my wallet - not my body.

Is the fact of the matter that the can represents a new type of product soon to be sharing the shelves with flourless bread, fruitless jam and grapeless wine? If so I think the public should be warned.

Doubtless you will respond in your inimitable style and certainly in a way which will terminate my brief flirtations with Tesco.

I look forward to hearing from you shortly and trust that in the meantime you are keeping well.

Yours sincerely

J. Grieg

<u>Jasper Griegson</u>

Our ref: 79845/rb

24 October 1997

Dear Mr Griegson

I am sorry to learn that a can of our Diet Classic Cola was empty.
David Sainsbury has asked me to apologise on his behalf and thank you
for letting us know about this.

As you know, quality is important to us and I am sorry that we have let
you down on this occasion. The can has been a great help in identifying
the batch involved and we will be following up this lapse with our
supplier. I hope this has not put you off buying our Classic Cola.

I have enclosed a voucher as a full refund for the can and I hope that
you will give us one more chance to serve you better.

I'd like to thank you again for telling us about this and I hope that you
will visit our stores again.

Yours sincerely

Terry Wells
Customer Services Director

Enc: £5 voucher

4
The Small Things in Life

Small is beautiful.

This is a maxim preached by many people wiser than myself. John Wayne Bobbit is perhaps the greatest exponent of the theory that size is not important but there are others (less procreatively-challenged than Mr Bobbit) who believe that this theory has a more general application.

I subscribe to the view that in everyday life it is the minutiae that count. It is said that if you look after the pennies, the pounds will look after themselves. There is a wider lesson to be learned from this maxim. If you can sort out the multitude of minor irritants that plague your life, the bigger problems will tend to fall by the wayside.

If you stop to think about it, happiness in this world is not index-linked to the BIG issues but rather to the tiny details. Is the Earth destined to be destroyed by a meteor in 2116? Does God exist? Will the Germans win the World Cup again?

These are not issues at the forefront of your mind while you wait in the queue at Sainsbury's. They are not even of much concern as you sit in the bath contemplating your navel. And even if they were, what difference would it make? It is not within your remit to marshal the wizardry of the world's top military scientists and create a meteor-busting nuclear warhead. Get real. Your job is to clean your navel, clean the bath and then sort out your life. By taking a grip on the things you can really affect you will feel surprisingly good about yourself. Try it.

Unfortunately we live in a world where mass delusion is the order of the day. The result of this is that most people are not only afraid to help themselves, they are totally incapable of doing so.

Take for example the masses who use the London Underground network every day. The trains (when they eventually arrive) are smelly, crowded and covered in nauseating graffiti. You're lucky if you arrive at your destination a mere 15 minutes late without having been flashed at or having had your pocket picked. The problems are so bad that the powers that be have been embarrassed into creating a 'Customer Charter'. The aggrieved commuter now has, it is suggested, a way to obtain compensation. He or she can fill out a blue form, complain about the late 8.06 from Northwood Hills and obtain a travel voucher worth £3.50. Whoopie! Spend, spend, spend.

Justice this ain't.

It is a pathetic sop-cum-opiate masquerading as Justice. It is London Transport's way of channelling the frustration of its long-suffering passengers into neat pigeon-holes where each person's grievance can be quietly and hygienically jettisoned in fragrant, disposable bin-liners. Are we really supposed to be content with a computer-generated apology and a voucher? The answer is that we are but the correct answer is that we should not be. Circumvent the system. Short circuit it. Next time your tube is delayed for 40 minutes in the tunnel between Baker Street and Great Portland Street take the voucher application form to your office, shred it and then wrap your brain around a letter written in blood to the

Metropolitan Line's General Manager, Charles Horton. He'll hate you. He hates the sight of blood. If you're really feeling bold you could carry out a company search, find his home address and send your letter at 3 am with a courier instructed to apologise for any inconvenience caused.

The plethora of 'Customer Charters' which have sprung up over the past few years have not heralded a new age of enlightenment where consumer rights are respected and honoured. *Au contraire.* They have created the mythology that multinational companies have formed a luvvy duvvy union with the Government and that by 'working together' we can make Britain a 'better place'. Crap. Customer charters are sedatives — designer drugs, carefully manufactured to pacify the wary user into sleepy submission. Like most drugs, customer charters should be avoided at all costs. If a company or organisation has inflicted a wrong upon you, you can hardly rely on that very entity's so-called complaints procedure to put things right. The only way forward is to flex your muscles as a free-thinking spirit. Be an individual. Companies hate individuals. They can't deal with them in the way they can deal with what market researchers call socio-economic groups. Individuals are not cost-effective – they are a pain in the backside. For this reason alone, it is advisable to be one.

ISAAC NEWTON'S REALLY BIG DISCOVERY:

16th October 1997

D.E. Young Esq
Deputy Chairman
John Lewis plc
171 Victoria Street
London SW1E 5NN

Dear Mr Young

My wife's a game old bird but there is a limit.

A few weeks ago she spent £3.95 at John Lewis on the enclosed "hold-ups". When she saw the word "hold-up" she assumed it meant elasticated stockings which require no suspenders. In fact "hold-up" would appear to allude to the daylight robbery suffered by the people unfortunate enough to by these dreadful garments. Put at its most basic the "hold-ups" do nothing of the sort. They drop like lead weights. The packaging referred to the colour as "barely navy". "Barely usable" would be a better description.

My wife discovered this fundamental flaw after donning her kit for a posh function last week-end. My beloved's aim of stunning her peers with suave glamour was, to say the least, somewhat thwarted as she hopped rabbit-like at half mast along the street.

Please ask your wife to try them out. You will then see what I mean. Do let me know how she get's on. Very badly I suspect.

I trust that having read this letter you will now leg it to your quality control boys office. I look forward to hearing from you.

Yours sincerely

J. Gray

Jasper Griegson

JOHN LEWIS PARTNERSHIP

20 October 1997
IFM/YSAQ/GI/4557L

171 Victoria Street
London   SW1E 5NN
Telephone (0171) 828 1000
Telex 8954150 Jonel G

Direct Line 0171 592 6288
Facsimile   0171 592 6294

Dear Mr Griegson

Mr Young has asked me to reply to your letter of 16 October, as I have a particular interest in customer concerns. I am very sorry the Charnos hold-ups didn't. Since the hosiery buying office is in this building, I have asked them to return the stockings to Charnos for testing. Of course there is no question that you should be out of pocket and John Lewis will be sending you, under separate cover, a cheque for £5, to cover the cost of the hold-ups and your trouble in returning them by post.

You have made no secret of the relish you take in composing an appropriately amusing letter setting out your own or others' troubles with the service world; and indeed I have enjoyed reading your intermittent exchanges with the Partnership. I must inescapably sound pompous in suggesting, however, that the amount of trouble you go to should really not be necessary. In this latest incident, while I cannot tell which Partnership shop you bought the stockings from in the first place, certainly your local branch, Trewins, would have been glad to refund the purchase price for you on the spot. That is, of course, the message that Mr Hampson set out in his letter to you of 28 August. Surely the time to start complaining is when we fail you at that fence, when your sallies will be more than justified.

Yours sincerely

Felicity Miller
Director

Our ref: L7554/IG/QASY/MFI
Your ref: IFM/YSAQ/GI/4557L

Felicity Miller
John Lewis Partnership
171 Victoria Street
London SW1E 5NN

Dear Felicity

Thank you for your letter of 20th October.

I feel honour-bound to respond to some of the points which you have made:-

☹ My wife is grateful for the fiver but 75 pence (after deducting postage) seems pitifully small compensation for the social embarrassment of shuffling like a lupine Nora Batty along the high street. How about a bar of chocolate in full and final settlement? That would do nicely.

☹ You suggest that my beloved should have returned to Trewins with the defective would-be stockings. Since the round trip would have taken at least an hour and would have involved the expense of parking and petrol it was far easier for me to drop your boss a line. Since you and Mr Hampson (may I call him Stuart?) have responded with such charm, politeness and speed, I know what I will be doing in future. Surely you can see my point of view?

☹ I would be grateful if you would let me see the results of the test to which you referred. I have written to the President of Du Pont in the USA and it will be interesting to swap notes.

It has in any event been a pleasure corresponding with you. If you write something funny you might even make it into my next book. Do keep in touch.

Yours sincerely

J. Grig

Jasper Griegson

JOHN LEWIS PARTNERSHIP

27 October 1997
IFM/YSAQ/GI/4561L

171 Victoria Street
London   SW1E 5NN
Telephone (0171) 828 1000
Telex 8954150 Jonel G

Direct Line 0171 592 6288
Facsimile   0171 592 6294

Dear Mr Griegson

I don't think I was as mean as all that. You have already demonstrated that you and your wife are flatteringly frequent visitors to a number of John Lewis shops. Had you simply waited until your next convenient trip, there would have been no extra cost, and I am confident that your reception in any of our hosiery departments would have been no less courteous. Neither you nor I would then have been spending expensive time in pursuing this entertaining correspondence, though my Monday morning in-tray would have been duller as a consequence.

Of course I have read your "How to" manual on complaining. I take issue with you on one point. If everyone with a minor difficulty were to accept your advice and start with the Chief Executive, not only would that demotivate (by bypassing) all of those at every stage down the line who might have been ready and willing to solve the problem; but also the sheer volume of straightforward and easy-to-settle concerns risks getting in the way of serious failures of performance being heard where they need to be. Nothing is more important to any trader's reputation than what happens to the customer at the front line, whether good or bad. If the Partnership were getting it so wrong that we could not handle the return of an item of make-up or a pair of stockings without making a drama out of it, then I would question whether we ought to be in business.

I have not yet heard from Charnos, other than to acknowledge receipt: when I do, I will let you know. Whatever might be wrong with the stockings, however, is unlikely to have anything to do with their lycra content.

Yours sincerely

Felicity Miller
Director

CHZ

30 October 1997

Felicity Miller
John Lewis Partnership
171 Victoria Street
London SW1E 5NN

Dear Felicity,

Thank you for your letter of 27th October 1997. I love it when you talk angry.

Yours sincerely

Jasper Griegson

Our ref: N0.B.\Ng

Felicity Miller
John Lewis Partnership
171 Victoria Street
London
SW1E 5NN

Dear Felicity

How are you? I hope you had a good break over the Yuletide
period. I didn't. I had a terrible break or rather my John Lewis
deluxe cracker had a terrible break – allow me to explain.

I sat at my dinner table with my family on Christmas day, poised to
enjoy our Christmas lunch. We started to pull some crackers and
all was jolly. Last but not least I pulled my cracker (with the aid of
my wife) only to discover that it was entirely devoid of a gift.
Imagine my horror. Whilst the other members of my family
proudly displayed their excellent gifts (including a superb shaving
brush and a charming brass padlock) I was left with bugger all.
My main fear is that my wife will interpret my dud cracker as a
damning indictment of my male prowess. My other fear is of
returning to Trewins in Watford, fighting for parking space, jostling
with the sales-hungry mob, queuing at the Customer Services
desk and then receiving a minuscule gesture of seasonal
goodwill.

I enclose the remains of the offending cracker and trust that you
will brighten up my new year with a wheelbarrow full of sympathy.

Best regards

Yours sincerely

J. Grig

Jasper Griegson

JOHN LEWIS PARTNERSHIP

05 January 1998
IFM/YSAQ/GI/4603L

171 Victoria Street
London SW1E 5NN
Telephone 071-828 1000
Telex 9419911/2 Jonel G

Direct Line 0171 592 6288
Facsimile   0171 592 6294

Dear Mr Griegson

Touché!

I have pleasure in enclosing gift vouchers to the value of the whole box of crackers, which can of course be spent on what you wish at any branch of the John Lewis Partnership or Waitrose and which I hope will mitigate your disappointment.

Yours sincerely

Felicity Miller (Miss)
Director

Enc. £30 GVs

Fernando Peire Esq.
The Ivy
1 West Street
London WC2H 9NE

Our ref: Poison Ivy

Dear Mr Peire

re: Dinner Disaster

I wish to register a complaint of the most serious kind.

Last Saturday night I treated some extremely high-powered business colleagues to what was supposed to be a meal at your restaurant. What we encountered was a calamity of Titanic proportions.

On our arrival you attempted to slash my wrists. After one of your self-detonating whisky glasses exploded in my hand I was shaken and stirred. Any suggestion that I was half cut at the time would be a misleading underestimate. I was lacerated.

You then attempted to mitigate my suffering by providing me with a pathetic blue plaster. Given that by this stage I needed a blood transfusion I need to say no more. I return the plaster but I suggest that you keep it safe since it will probably be needed as an exhibit at the trial. Moreover, you then attempted to placate me with an exquisite perfectly-chilled bottle of champagne. Let us treat that act as irrefutable admission of liability.

As if all this were not too dreadful for words you than capped it all. You placed a few tables away from us Radio Two's equivalent of saturation bombing:

Des O'Connor.

My colleagues and I spent the entire meal fearing that at any moment Des might burst into song. Our peace of mind, our palates and our digestion all suffered irreversible damage. By way of compensation I would be most grateful indeed for my bodyweight in chocolate buttons.

I look forward to hearing from you.

Yours sincerely

J. Grig

Jasper Griegson

P.D. Kindersley Esq
Chairman
Dorling Kindersley Holdings plc
9 Henrietta Street
London WC2E 8PS

31 October 1997

Dear Mr Kindersley

I wish to register a complaint.

My wife and I are firm believers in the benefits of educational software and there can be little doubt that your company produces some of the finest material for small children. Having recently invested in *My First Incredible Amazing Dictionary* for our five year old daughter we discovered to our horror a definition so incorrect that it is truly incredible and amazing.

A witch is defined as:-

> 'An imaginary woman with magical powers'

This is wholly inaccurate. As the Pagan Federation of Great Britain will doubtless tell you, witches are anything but imaginary. You can fax them on 01691-671066. They do not have black hats, broomsticks, warts, green skin or hooked noses. Some are housewives, others are doctors, teachers, secretaries and so on.

If you would like to meet some witches my wife would be only too delighted to make the necessary arrangements. Please note that this will only take a couple of phone calls. It will not involve frogs, blood or poisonous apples.

My daughter is confused. Please restore her faith and mine in the quality of your products.

Yours sincerely

J. Grig

Jasper Griegson

28th November 1997

Dear Mr Griegson

Thank you for your letter of 27th November . Unfortunately your letter of 31st October never reached me, thus the delay in replying.

I am sorry that you are disappointed with our definition of a witch as *an imaginary woman with magical powers*. I am afraid whether we like it or not most people do not believe in magic let alone magical powers, therefore by definition witches are imaginary.

Yours sincerely

Peter Kindersley
Chairman

Charles Horton Esq
General Manager
Metropolitan Line
London Underground Limited

Dear Charles

I apologise for any inconvenience caused but I thought I should write to you about a Metropolitan Line problem. I have no doubt that you will want to help me and several hundred other commuters who travel into London from Northwood every day.

Allow me to explain.

Anyone who leaves from Northwood bound for Baker Street, Kings Cross, Farringdon, Barbican or Moorgate (ie.an awful lot of people) will wait at the extreme south end of the platform since this is where the exit is at those stations. I have been doing this for some eleven years and will probably continue to do so for several decades to come. The problem is that there is no bench at this end of the platform. Me and my fellow passengers (who often find that delays and cancelled trains prolong the wait) would love to have somewhere to park our bums other than on the cold, lumpy, uncomfortable wall which surrounds the flower bed.

In order to help you consider our plight I would be grateful if you would take the following into account:-

1) On the assumption that I will work for the next thirty years, continue to live in Northwood and wait on average 10 minutes each day, I calculate that I may spend a total of 11,000 hours standing when I could be sitting.

2) My depressed state at this prospect is reflected in a very accurate picture drawn by my daughter Nina a copy of which is attached.

3) I have a spare bench in my garden. You can have that if you like.

I look forward to hearing from you. Some time before the year 2027 would be preferable. If you would like to meet next to the flower-bed one morning please let me know.

Yours sincerely   J Gily

Circle line

Ext/Direct
Our ref
Your ref
Date

0171 918 1704
120/DW/8537

27 March, 1997

London Underground Limited
13 Allsop Place
London NW1 5LJ
Telephone 0171·918 2069

Dear Mr Greigson,

Thank you for your letter of 24th March concerning re-positioning of a bench from north to southbound platform at Northwood station.

I am pleased to hear that the matter has satisfactorily been resolved by Ian Harriss and that the bench should be moved within the next few weeks. I will ensure that your thanks are passed on to him.

Yours sincerely,

Charles Horton
General Manager
Metropolitan and Circle Lines

Paul Walden Esq
The Flying Music Group plc
FM House
110 Clarendon Road
London W11 2HR

20th March 1997

Dear Mr Walden

I wish to register a complaint of the most serious kind.

Last night my wife and I went to see the Monkees 30th anniversary concert at Wembley Arena. Our tickets cost forty-six pounds in all (see the attached) and we were deeply disappointed for a number of spurious reasons including the following.

As a prelude to the Monkees arrival on stage a video was shown featuring the famous song *Hey, Hey, We're the Monkees*. This number included the following words:-

> *"We're the **young generation** and we've got something to say"*

I hate to be pernickety but the ***young generation*** they were not. The boys had been well preserved with a blast of embalming fluid and perhaps a touch of hormone replacement therapy but to describe them as the ***young generation*** was a gross and fraudulent misrepresentation.

I would be most grateful if you could arrange for each member of the group to provide my wife and I with a written apology, a cheque for forty-six quid and an assurance that the two offending words will in future be replaced with something like ***old geriatrics***. This would scan nicely and has the unimpeachable virtue of accuracy.

If the Monkees are not too frail to pick up a pen, I look forward to hearing from them.

Yours sincerely

J. Griey

Jasper Griegson

PS. We enjoyed the concert immensely. Congratulations on an excellent production!

25th March 1997

Our Ref: Deborah/jg-23-3-97

Dear Mr Griegson

Thank you for your letter of the 20th of March last detailing your complaints about the Monkees Concert in London. As all of the matters that you mention require direct input from the group themselves, I will of course pass on your letter for response.

Yours sincerely

Paul Walden
JOINT MANAGING DIRECTOR
THE FLYING MUSIC COMPANY LIMITED

P.S. Due to their advancing years and the speed that they are able to function these days, it may be some time before you receive the benefit of a reply from them.

P.P.S. I'm glad that you enjoyed the concert and thank you for you kind note.

Your ref: Deborah/jg-23-3-97

31 March 1997

Paul Walden Esq
The Flying Music Group plc
FM House
110 Clarendon Road
London W11 2HR

Dear Paul

Thank you very much for your letter of 25th March.

If the Monkees reply then I'm a believer.

Yours sincerely

J. Grieg

Jasper Griegson

PRIVATE & CONFIDENTIAL

N.D. Cadbury Esq
Group Chief Executive
Cadbury Schweppes PLC
1 Connaught Place
London
W2

19th October 1988

Dear Sir

RE: The Flake

I have always thought that only the crumbliest, flakiest
chocolate tastes like chocolate never tasted before. Despite
giving full weight to that crucial assumption, I have been
forced to write to you and to register a complaint. Flakes have
changed and I do not like the alteration one little bit. As you
will note from the enclosed wrapper, my dissatisfaction has not
resulted from any variation in the chocolate itself but rather
from a modification to the Flake's famous yellow packaging. As
you must be aware, the Flake always used to be lagged by an
easy-to-unwrap sheet. One of the few pleasures left open to
Modern Man was to eat a Flake and then... and this is crucial...
to make a funnel out of the paper, tip it up in the air and
swallow the crumbs. Those days are over. The new style wrapper
has been designed in the form of a sealed sheath. It is more
akin to a surgical dressing than a wrapper. I do not wish to
consume my favourite chocolate bar out of a hideous cocoon. The
shroud of the Flake is a garment to be respected.

I look to you for a crumb of comfort and an option to purchase
all remaining stocks of Flakes in their traditional wrappers.

Yours faithfully

Jasper Griegson

CADBURY LTD.

the first name in chocolate

PO BOX 12
BOURNVILLE
BIRMINGHAM B30 2LU
TELEPHONE 021-458 2000
TELEX 338011 LINDE
FACSIMILE (GP III) 021-458 2660

V54/CS/MGC

27th October 1988

Dear Mr Griegson

Your letter to Mr N D Cadbury has been passed to us at Bournville.

I am sorry that the "Flow-pack" wrapper on the Flake is causing you some displeasure when trying to enjoy the chocolate.

As this is made at our Dublin factory I have been in touch with them concerning your disappointment. I understand that the reason for this type of pack is that it is used for Selection Packs and Multi-packs were extra handling is involved. Some Consumer trials were carried out before this was put into production.

However, not all is lost because your favourite "Twist-wrap" Flake is still in production and I hope you will enjoy the samples sent to you under separate cover.

We trust you will continue to purchase our products in the future and thank you for your interest in bringing this to our attention.

Yours sincerely

M G Chadderton
Consumer Services Manager

Chris Burrell Esq
Unwin Seeds Limited
Histon
Cambridge
CB4 4LE

26th August 1997

Dear Mr Burrell

I wish to register a complaint.

I write on behalf of my geriatric parents who decided last
Saturday to forgo their lottery ticket in favour of a superbly
priced packet of your *Blue Cloud* forget-me-not seeds. For a
mere 99 pence they thought that they would become the proud
owners of some gorgeous flowers. The seeds, it seemed, were a
far better investment than a five minute financial fantasy coupled
with a glimpse of the shining gnashers of Anthea Turner or
whoever her replacement is.

My parents were wrong.

Their packet (copy enclosed) contained a mere four seeds.
Forget me what! Is there a world seed shortage or something?

In any event, at 25 pence a seed it would seem that I am in the
wrong business – you must be making an absolute packet on
every packet. In fact you definitely making an absolute packet –
one without enough seeds in it.
On the assumption that my parents were lucky and all four seeds
germinate as planned, their flower bed will still look pretty
weedy.

I trust that it is within your discretion to exercise some flower
power and make my parents' day by compensating them. Given
that they could have won millions on the lottery I trust that you
will be suitably generous.

I await your earliest reply.

Yours sincerely

J. Grigson

Jasper Griegson

Unwins Seeds Limited
Histon, Cambridge CB4 4LE, England
Telephone: 01 223 236 236 24 Hours
Fax: 01 223 237 437

29 August 1997

Dear Mr Griegson

Thank you for your letter regarding your seeds, we were sorry to learn of your disappointing experience with our seeds and can appreciate the inconvenience this packaging error has caused you.

Thank you for bringing this to our attention, we will be investigating this error. To date we have had no similar complaints.

I enclose a replacement packet of seeds for your parents with our apologies for the inconvenience caused.

Yours sincerely

Mary Marsters

Mary Marsters
Gardening Adviser

5

Why Computers Don't Work

We live in an imperfect world.

The English scientist J.B.S. Haldane was once asked what inferences could be drawn about the nature of God from a study of his works. His reply was that God must have an inordinate fondness of beetles.

The short but accurate truth is that the world is not composed of neat logically interlocking boxes. It is rough at the edges, lumpy in patches and on a scale of one to ten scores ten for irregularity. Human beings attempt, rather pathetically, to impose order in the place of natural anarchy. On the whole these efforts end in failure. The starting point for a more focused view of the world is to understand the chaos. Anything that can go wrong will go wrong and will do so right in the middle of your favourite television programme.

Consider the so-called advance of technology.

There are those who believe that technology will make for a more orderly world. They are deluding themselves. Technology makes for a more chaotic world. There is a simple reason for this: no one really understands it and those that do are useless at explaining themselves. Computers are the best examples of non-functioning technology. They don't work. There are many reasons for this.

First, all computers secrete voluminous multi-coloured wires and do so with unnatural profusion. The result is that sooner or later the computer's user trips over the heap of electronic arteries and pulls the computer's umbilical cord from its socket.

The second reason is that computers are not built by computers. They are built by men. Worse still, the men in question are not necessarily the finest examples that homo sapiens as a species has to offer. They are usually dull anorak types who misspent their youth by going to Sheffield University to study physics where they drank watered down beer at the Union Bar and cooked chips in lard. Why, you may ask, do companies allow the software for their multimillion pound databases to be created by inept males, 90% of whose bodies and brains comprise a glutinous combination of pot noodles, congealed animal fat and Worthingtons bitter?

The third reason is that when computers go wrong they cannot be fixed. If you ask ten software engineers to fix a light bulb they will look at you blankly, charge you £300 plus VAT, consult the manual, ring up head office and then tell you that they cannot fix lightbulbs. Fixing lightbulbs is a hardware problem.

To be a really good complainer you have to rejoice in the fact that things don't work. Perfection is an illusion. Most things in the world just hang together and not very well at that. Note the following:-

- The tomatoes in Burger King's hamburgers do not bear the shimmering scarlet colour depicted in the advertisements. Let's face it: they are a dull red. It's called reality.
- Within six months no washing machine looks like the one in the brochure. It soon clogs up with horrible soapy bits and limescale deposits and then sticks two fingers up at your steaming pile of soiled underwear by snapping

its fanbelt as a gesture of defiance just as you've returned home from a three week vacation.

- The sun does not shine in Crete. Not when you're there on holiday. It's windy and cloudy and,what the hell, the airline lost the suitcase in which you kept your swimming costume and towel.
- If it can go wrong it will go wrong and will do so with astonishingly bad timing. Discount for the mismanaged disarray and you are half way to forming a better, clearer view of the world. Once you've done this, you can then set about sorting out the crummy bits.

NICHOLAS SHEPHERD ESQ
MANAGING DIRECTOR
BLOCKBUSTER ENTERTAINMENT LTD
45 RIVERSIDE WAY
UXBRIDGE
MIDDLESEX UB8 2YF

THE COMPLAINER

21 JANUARY 1997

DEAR MR SHEPHERD

RE: A BLOCKBUSTER PENALTY

SOMEWHERE WITHIN YOUR OFFICES AT UXBRIDGE THERE IS A COMPUTER. I DON'T KNOW WHAT IT LOOKS LIKE BUT I SUSPECT ITS ONE OF THOSE GHASTLY 1960'S JOBS. YOU KNOW THE TYPE - LARGE AND SILVER WITH AN ARRAY OF WHIRRING REEL TO REEL TAPES, MULTICOLOURED FLASHING LIGHTS AND CHEAP PLASTIC KNOBS. FOR EASE OF REFERENCE LET'S CALL THIS GREAT THRESHING MACHINE OF CYBERNETIC INTELLECT *BOB THE BRAIN*.

BOB IS PRESUMABLY AGEING A BIT AND PROBABLY NEEDS A 100,000 MB SERVICE. I WOULD HAVE THOUGHT THAT AT THE VERY LEAST HIS HARD DISK COULD DO WITH A RUBBING DOWN, HIS CHIPS COULD DO WITH SOME OIL AND HIS RAM COULD DO WITH A RAM UP THE C DRIVE. I SAY THIS BECAUSE BOB IS NOT PERFORMING WELL. IN FACT BOB IS PERFORMING SO BADLY THAT HE IS GENERATING OFFENSIVE GARBAGE AN EXAMPLE OF WHICH I ATTACH.

HAVING BEEN A LOYAL MEMBER OF THE BLOCKBUSTER VIDEO SHOP SINCE ITS INCEPTION I RESENT BEING SENT THREATENING LETTERS DEMANDING THE PRINCELY SUM OF 50 PENCE IN CIRCUMSTANCES WHERE I PAID THE SAID 50 PENCE THREE MONTHS AGO! I HAVE NEVER HAD ANY PROBLEMS WITH YOUR COMPANY IN THE PAST AND I CAN ONLY SUPPOSE THAT BOB WROTE THIS LETTER HAVING BEEN INFECTED BY THE MYSTERIOUS COMPUTER VIRUS KNOWN AS "POISON PEN FLU".

PLEASE LET ME KNOW WHAT ON EARTH IS GOING ON. NO OFFENCE TO BOB BUT I WOULD LIKE TO HEAR FROM YOU.

YOURS SINCERELY

J. Grieg

BLOCKBUSTER ENTERTAINMENT LIMITED
European Headquarters
45 Riverside Way
Uxbridge, Middlesex UB8 2YF
Telephone: 01895 258866
Fax No: 01895 272062

6 February 1997

Dear Mr Griegson

Thank you for your note. I was most taken with your somewhat accurate and graphic description of myself and I thoroughly endorse your suggestion of a 100,000 MB service (although the kind people at Blockbuster do look after me well, normally).

Nick Shepherd has shown me your letter and I must confess it was not me who in fact wrote to you, it was one of my users who failed in this instance to notice the meagre amount outstanding on your account, something we would normally never enter into writing to collect. Unfortunately, in this instance, it was, in fact, a human error!

I know everyone here hopes that no offence was taken as this was an oversight and must have appeared somewhat impolite, but these humans do tend to do this from time to time. I have suggested that we enter upon your account a number of free rentals in order to demonstrate how all of us (machines and people!) are sorry for sending you such a note. I hope you will accept this as a token of our appreciation of your custom.

Thank you for taking the time and trouble to write to Mr. Shepherd, who I know fully concurs with my own view on this matter.

Regards and Best Wishes

BOB

David Hamid, Esq
Managing Director
Mastercare Limited
Maylands Court
Maylands Avenue
Hemel Hempstead
Herts, HP2 7DG

ipcmagazines

16 January 1995

Dear David

<u>Hot Currys Are Good But Hotpoints From Currys Are Not</u>

How are you? Only last week I was singing your praises on London Newstalk Radio (I am now their Official Complainer too). I cited you as living proof that the Man at the Top cares. You should be paying me to say such things!

As you will see from the heading to this letter I have turned my hand to moral philosophy. The inspiration for this mental masterpiece has been a complaint by Mrs K Rosenfeld

Mrs Rosenfeld's dilemma is somewhat simpler than the mathematical paradoxes with which Pythagorus tortured himself or the intractable political questions with which Kant, Nietzsche and then Marx wrestled.

Mrs Rosenfeld's problem is that her Hotpoint 7823P dishwasher is a duffer. Since buying it brand new on 9 August 1994 (policy number 7245923/CRY) Mrs Rosenfeld has had more than enough cause to do wht the last three letters of her policy number indicate.

The plastic on the top panel has chipped off and there is a crack of earthquake proportions running from top to bottom on the right hand side. Each time she closes the door the crack splits further. In addition, the tray keeps falling off its hinges each time she pulls it out!!

A succession of Hotpoint servicemen have been round but to no avail. The latest has just cancelled his appointment.

Mrs Rosenfeld does not wish to entertain any more men in boiler suits. She wants a dishwasher that works. In the meantime she has had to revert to taps, a washing up bowl and squeezy.

If René Descartes had been a dishwasher doubtless he would have said:-

"I'm not a sink, therefore I am"

Dishwashers are supposed to wash dishes (yet more philosophy). Please wave your magic dish cloth and make Mrs Rosenfeld's wish come true. She wants a replacement and she wants it NOW.

I await your earliest reply.

Best wishes.

Yours sincerely

<u>Jasper Griegson</u>

MASTERCARE
Putting Customers First

SERVICE AND INSTALLATION

FOR

DIXONS AND CURRYS

Mr Jasper Griegson
IPC Magazines Limited
King's Reach Tower
Stamford Street
London SE1 9LS

17th January 1995

Dear Jasper

It's great to hear from you again and congratulations on getting the London Newstalk Radio job: I'm delighted things are going so well for you. Thanks for saying nice things about me on the radio I am really touched that someone in your position would take the trouble. You will definitely get a chocolate biscuit with your coffee next time you come to see me.

I've been investigating the problem of Mrs Rosenfeld's dishwasher and you are quite right, she should not have to put up with all this inconvenience with a virtually new machine. Fortunately Hotpoint take the same view and have agreed to replace it for her. They will contact her and arrange a convenient time for delivery. Yet another happy customer!

Incidentally, I never thanked you for the kind gift of your very entertaining book. That was very remiss of me and I apologise. Actually it has given me a few ideas for complaining to a few companies myself. Who knows you may be hearing from me from 'the other side of the fence' as it were.

Very best wishes for the New Year.

Yours sincerely

David Hamid

(P.S I enjoyed the Descartes "quote")

David Hamid
MANAGING DIRECTOR

2 January 1996

M Souhami
Deputy Chairman
Dixons Group plc
29 Farm Street
London, W1X 7RD

Dear Souhami

I am London Newstalk Radio's Official Complainer and I write on behalf of Mr Howard Rosen whose letter to me is enclosed for ease of reference. I would like to summarise the position as follows:-

> *"Mr Rosen is the owner*
> *Of an 18 month old CD*
> *Which he acquired from a Dixons branch*
> *For a rather costly fee.*
>
> *The problem is that astonishingly*
> *The machine is beyond repair*
> *Which after such a short-lived span*
> *Seems anything but fair.*
>
> *He didn't expect to come away*
> *From a visit to Brent Cross*
> *With a useless lump of mechanical*
> *Electronic dross.*
>
> *This saga has seemed interminable*
> *But I trust that now you will*
> *Spring into action with some justice*
> *And a gesture of goodwill."*

I look forward to hearing from you.

Yours sincerely

Jasper Griegson

Dixons Stores Group

Maylands Avenue
Hemel Hempstead
Herts HP2 7TG
Telephone: 01442 353000
Fax: 01442 233218
Telex: 934594

Please quote : KL SK 610820/VP

Mr J Griegson
London Radio Services Ltd
72 Hammersmith Road
London
W14 8YE

22 February 1996

Dear Mr Griegson

Thank you for your letter addressed to our Chairman regarding your earlier correspondence to our company on behalf of Mr Rosen.

Please accept my apologies for the fact you have not been replied to regarding this matter, however I can confirm that contact was made with Mr Rosen following your letter to Mr Souhami and the matter brought to a satisfactory conclusion. I enclose a copy of our letter to Mr Rosen dated the 19th January outlining our offer of settlement to him.

Yours sincerely

KAREN LASHLEY
EXECUTIVE, CHAIRMAN'S OFFICE

Our ref: FAB 1

27th April 1990

The Legal Director
Tandon Limited
Hunt End
Redditch
Worcs

Dear Sir

Re: International Rescue v Tandon Limited

I write on behalf of my client (hereinafter referred to as "Brains"), a copy of whose photograph your company is currently using as part of a commercial advertising campaign.

I have advised Brains that your use of his photograph (copy attached) constitues a gross defamation of his character and that accordingly he is entitled to claim exemplary damages in proceedings against you. The text of the advertisement suggests that Brains is:-

a) a dummy and
b) manipulated by strings.

Both these scurrilous imputations are of course completely without foundation. Far from being stupid or incapable of independent thought, Brains is nothing less than a genius of Einsteinian proportions. Never mind his stutter, think of his intellect in the "Sun Probe" and "Day of Disaster" missions. In the light of the above Brains looks to you for compensation in the following form:-

1) a published written apology to Jeff and the boys
2) a lifetime supply of FAB ice-lollies (bet you can't remember them)
3) a pink Rolls Royce.

I await your prompt response.

Yours faithfully

J. Griey

Jasper Griegson

**S P D
C&J**

May 1 1990

Dear Mr Griegson

I write on behalf of the advertising agency who developed the advertisement using 'Brains'.

We have given your letter the most serious consideration and feel the best 'compensation' we can offer your Client is the enclosed photograph of himself (otherwise known as the advertisement).

We believe 'Brains' looks most attractive in the advertisement and will be pleased to see himself so represented.

We thank you for your concern and interest (and no, we can't remember FAB ice-lollies).

Yours sincerely

Julie Leese

JULIE LEESE
Account Manager

enc.

6

Complainers of
the World

As I said at the start of this book, the British are pretty awful at complaining. What of our brethren in other countries? Are they any good?

The Germans
The Germans are not good at complaining. The main reason for this is the profound inhibiting effect of constipation on the entire Teutonic race. Years of bratwurst and pumpernickel consumption have taken their toll on the nation's regularity. As a result the Germans are so bunged up and frustrated that they can barely speak, let alone complain.

There are other reasons however for the German unwillingness to complain.

For starters, there is nothing to complain about. The 9.03 train from Munich to Essen leaves at 9.03; the leaves fall from the trees at noon on 1st October each year; the Lowenbrau is excellent; the autobahns are excellent; the towns are modern, *very modern*; the cars never need repairing and anyone who disagrees with any of the above has long since been silenced with piano wire.

Another reason for the Germans' reticence is that when

it comes to authority they are even worse than the English. They don't fear authority, they respect authority. If it has been stamped with a red seal or if it wears a smart uniform it is part of the natural order of things and is therefore good. If a German went into a restaurant and saw his smoked herring pâté incorrectly recorded in the menu as a main course he would not complain. As all John Cleese fans know, hors d'oeuvres are hors d'oeuvres.

When the Germans do however get a real bee in their bonnet they tend to go for it big time. Rather than mess around with polite letters to Customer Services they will spend seven years building up their military strength and then eradicate the problem with a thousand bomber raid. When push comes to shove, what the Germans lack in subtlety they more than compensate for with buckets of testosterone.

The Italians

The Italian weather means that the Italians are not hindered by British-style reserve. On the contrary, the Italians (who have never worked) spend each and every day swanning around in sunny cafes, waving their arms and getting their points of view across to their fellow men. They all know how to complain and there is no shortage of things to complain about. The 9.03 train from Pisa to Florence has never left at 9.03. The timetable shows that it is due to leave at 9.24, it sometimes leaves at 9.37 and it has only once ever arrived on time and that was because the wife of Massimo (the driver) was about to give birth.

Although the Italians complain a lot in the sense that they gesticulate a fair bit, they do not write letters. The Italian postal service is less reliable than a carrier pigeon on Benzedrine and even if the letter does make it to the Customer Services Department at Fiat's head office, there

isn't much point because the Customer Services Department at Fiat's head office doesn't exist.

In 1977 one foolish man decided to take matters to the top by complaining to the Chairman of Fiat about the fact that his car was starting to rust after only two years. The person should have been overjoyed at the fact that the engine had lasted that long, let alone the body work. Nevertheless he was not content and pursued his complaint to the highest authority in the company. He was last seen being escorted late one night into a top of the range black Fiat from where he was taken to the Italy's equivalent of Clarks: Francos — the concrete boot fitters.

The Australians

It has been said that Australia is the country where men are men, women are women and sheep are nervous. Anyone dealing with an irate Australian consumer also needs to be pretty nervous. Like the Germans, the Australians possess about as much subtlety as a kick in the nether regions. As is plain from the modest nature of Australia's contribution to classic world literature (ie. nil) the men from Down Under don't write a lot down. When an Australian is pissed off about the temperature of his beer he is far more likely to head butt the person serving it than he is to compose a carefully constructed letter to the chairman of the brewery. Consumer disputes in Australia are sorted out in the same way as political and indeed legal disputes: the respective parties exchange glances and then fight it out with fisticuffs in a pub somewhere. Occasionally there is a process whereby mediation and arbitration takes place and the parties concerned discuss the matter like adults and come to a sensible settlement – only joking ... the kangaroos occasionally do this but the humans never do. There's nothing like a good brawl. Anything else is for woosies.

The Indians

India is a time warp. The Indians have red pillar boxes, a newspaper called *The Times*, steam trains with the word 'Sheffield' written on the side and cigarette packets identical to those sold in England in 1938. The worst part about India is that still bears the bureaucratic hallmarks of British colonial rule. The cities of India are cluttered with sprawling ramshackle offices, each one overmanned to a degree of about 600% Notwithstanding the vast numbers of people apparently available to sort things out, nothing, absolutely nothing, ever gets done. This means that if you have a problem it will eventually be resolved in the same way as all other problems in India – you will grow old and die and the problem will be forgotten.

For those foolish enough not to appreciate that a very long period of time (eternity to be precise) is something which must be endured in all situations involving adversity, the battle against the tide inevitably proves fruitless. Letters written to the headquarters of India's most

respected companies are not lost but retained in rotting yellow heaps which go back to 1953. They are unlikely to be dealt with this side of the year 3000. Those who take matters further by visiting the company in question become sucked into a bureaucratic vortex which ultimately involves waiting in a queue. The queue of course has no beginning and no end. The lot of the aggrieved Indian consumer is not a happy one.

The Americans

Since the vast majority of Americans are trigger-happy litigation lawyers there is no doubt that the Americans are the best complainers on this side of the Solar System. The Americans thrive on a diet of raw meat and powdered glass for breakfast followed by an acrimonious and bitter legal dispute for lunch. They love confrontation. They may be told to 'have a nice day' every five minutes but they rarely do unless having a nice day involves sustaining a grievous personal injury at the expense of an insurance company.

The Americans are brash and uninhibited and complaining comes very naturally to them. The American psyche on this front stems from the Wild West spirit which has mutated into something every bit as aggressive but much uglier. The gunslingers have been replaced by sharp-suited lawyers and the battleground is no longer the plains of Texas but rather the US legal system.

Why do Americans complain so much? The answer is that they expect quality in all products and services. The tragic truth is that they are surprisingly devoted to absolutely dreadful consumer items. For example, take McDonalds – please, do us all a favour, *take* McDonalds. The two important things for the Americans are (1) that they think they're getting the tip top best of everything (even though they're not) and (2) that they will take

disproportionately radical action when they perceive that something has gone wrong. It is a well known fact that the Vietnam war started following a dispute about a portion of sweet and sour chicken in a Chinese take-away on 5th Avenue. It is a lesser known fact that 95 per cent of all complaints in America are about food and of those 95 per cent are the same: the portions weren't big enough. This remarkable statistic lies at the heart of the San Andreas fault which runs through the moral fibre of American society: the portions are big enough, it's just that they're not big enough for the average elephantine American. In short therefore, the Americans complain all the time but have nothing to complain about.

The French

When it comes to a discussion about complaining the French will always rear their ugly heads. This is not because the French are good at complaining as such. In fact they are not good at complaining at all. What they are good at is striking.

Very few people have ever been to France. Millions have tried. Some get close but few make it. The reason for this is twofold. First, since 1965 there has been a permanent strike of French Air Traffic Control. This strike has peaks and troughs but it is always there and it becomes particularly heated on frantic bank holiday weekends. The strike may peter out when the hardline strikers (many of them now in their late eighties) go to the Great Control Tower in the Sky but until then the strike is here to stay. Secondly, any attempt to penetrate the French mainland by tunnel or ferry then road is as doomed to failure as an airborne assault. This is because all French motorways are blocked by in-bred French farmers and their sheep. Like the French Air Traffic Controllers, the Protesting French Farmers are as much a part of French life as the Eiffel Tower, chocolate croissants and the Marseillaise. The Protesting French

GARÇON, ZERE EES A FLY EEN MY SOUP. I WEEL NOT EAT IT. EEN FACT I WEEL NOT EAT ANYFING. I WEEL STRIKE!

Farmers have long since forgotten what they are complaining about. Like their sheep, they just do what comes naturally and follow each other around in moping flocks. Occasionally they will champion a particular cause – one minute it's mad cow disease the next minute its cheap imports of Dutch lamb. It doesn't matter. Their objective is always the same namely to thwart any attempt by any foreigner to penetrate further inland than Pierre's Greasy Spoon Cafe at Calais. They are so successful that any more detailed research into the behaviour of the French is impossible.

The Chinese

In China there are no complaints.

The Swiss

The Swiss are perhaps the most civilised of all complainers. They resolve all their disputes by way of a protracted but peaceful arbitration process at meetings in beautiful hotels and conference rooms overlooking Lake Geneva. Usually the subject matter of disputes in Switzerland (which is even more perfect than Germany) is so dull and anodyne that the winner tends to be the person with the highest boredom threshold. The last bust-up to reach the Swiss Courts concerned the unusually elliptical shape of five holes in a 2 kilogram batch of Gruyère.

The Swiss of the 1990s could spend their time far more profitably if they reverted to their ancient form of dispute resolution which involved no more than twenty minutes, a tree, an apple and a crossbow. The reason that they don't do this any longer is that the Swiss have very little to do in their perfect lives other than sterilise their piles of cash with antiseptic polish, sterilise the floors of Zurich Airport, visit health farms and watch the time with great precision.

Marco Pierre-White
The Criterion
Piccadilly
London W1

THE COMPLAINER

1st February 1997

Dear Marco

A few weeks ago my wife and I treated ourselves and six friends to an excellent meal at your above-mentioned restaurant.

The atmosphere was both congenial and vibrant. The food was succulent, fragrant and yet at the same time deliciously sophisticated. The service capped it all: the waiters managed to combine unobtrusiveness with efficiency - a rare and special art.

Notwithstanding all of these qualities the occasion was marred by a detail which I can only imagine will horrify you.

When it came to coffee one of the items on the menu described itself as EXPRESSO. As a lover of the Italian language, the Italian people and Italian cuisine I am fairly sure than the correct spelling is ESPRESSO. I enclose a copy of the relevant extract from the pretty definitive *Collins Italian Dictionary*. Doubtless you will want to take a quick butchers at the menu to double check my observation.

I would be most grateful indeed for your comments.

Yours sincerely

J. Griep

Jasper Griegson

espresso (p.p. di esprimere) I a. 1 (manifesto) express, explicit
sono venuto per tuo ~ desiderio I have come at your express
wish. 2 (veloce, rapido) express, fast: treno ~ express train. 3 inv.
(Post) express, (am) special delivery~: lettera ~ express letter. II
s.m. 1 (lettera espresso) express letter, (am) special delivery
letter; (francobollo espresso) express stamp, (am) special
delivery stamp; (scritta sulle lettere) Express, (am) Special
Delivery. 2 (Ferr) (treno espresso) express (train). 3 (caff
espresso) espresso. □ per ~ by express, (am) by special delivery
consegna per ~ express; spedire una lettera per ~ to send a lette
express; piatto ~ dish cooked upon request.

THE CRITERION BRASSERIE
MARCO PIERRE WHITE

March 11th 1997.

Dear Mr Griegson,

Thank you for your letter. I read your comments with interest. We have now acted on your recommendation and rectified the situation.

Yours sincerely,

Marco Pierre White

12th March 1997

Marco Pierre White
The Criterion Brasserie
Piccadilly
London W1V 9LB

Dear Marco

Thank you for your kind letter of 11 March.

I am so impressed that I will be returning this Saturday with my wife and two important business associates.

I am delighted that in every department you continue to treat perfection as your primary objective. Do join us for coffee if you're not too busy boiling courgettes in the kitchen.

Yours sincerely

Jasper Griegson

18th March 1997

Antonio Raillo Esq
General Manager
The Criterion Brasserie
224 Piccadilly
London W1V 9LB

Dear Mr Raillo

Following the recent important changes to your menu I returned last Saturday to your restaurant with two highly valued business associates (see copy bill attached). The food was absolutely excellent - I particularly enjoyed the black forest gateau followed by a deliciously aromatic double espresso coffee.

I am not of a nervous disposition but unfortunately our guests are and their meal was marred by a somewhat bizarre incident. Seated a mere ten feet away from us was Mr Salman Rushdie. My guests rather gobbled the superb cuisine fearing that at any moment the restaurant would be sprayed with machine-gun fire or blown up.

Accustomed as I am to low-fatwa food I was totally unperturbed. In somewhat stark contrast however my guests' digestion was deeply upset. Had the neighbouring table been occupied by Ian Paisley, or worse, Michael Winner, the effects could have been catastrophic.

In the circumstances I would be most grateful if you could provide my guests with the Mother of all apologies.

I repeat that apart from this curious divertissement the meal was absolutely first-class and well worthy of a return visit.

I look forward to hearing from you.

Yours sincerely

J. Grieg

Jasper Griegson

Sir Paul Condon
Metropolitan Police
New Scotland Yard
Broadway
London SW1H 0BG

22nd March 1997

Dear Sir Paul

I would be most grateful indeed for your assistance with the following problem.

Last Saturday night (15th March) I went to the Criterion Restaurant in Piccadilly and had a thoroughly enjoyable meal. In the course of scoffing my grub I noticed that on the table next to me sat Salman Rushdie.

I have always been a great admirer of Salman's work, particularly *Midnight's Children*, and I was desperately keen to get his autograph. Every time I began to edge towards Salman's table however I received extremely dirty looks from the six people sitting with him. They appeared to be plain clothes cops from special branch - I could tell this from their funny moustaches, the holes in the middle of the newspapers they were pretending to read and their bulging gun-shaped pockets. I decided, on balance, to steer well clear fearing that any approach might have resulted in a verbal altercation coupled with an unpleasant spray of machine-gun fire.

In the circumstances I wonder if you could have a word with the officer in charge of operation fatwa and see whether or not he might be able to get Salman's autograph for me by a safer route.

I thank you in advance for your assistance and look forward to hearing from you.

Yours sincerely

Jasper Griegson

Date: 25 March 1997

METROPOLITAN POLICE SERVICE
Strategic Co-ordination Group

New Scotland Yard
Broadway
London SW1H 0BG

Dear Mr Griegson

I write to acknowledge receipt of your letter dated 22 March 1997 addressed to the Commissioner, received in this office on the 25 March 1997.

I regret to inform you that we are unable to assist you in obtaining the autograph of Salman Rushdie and would suggest that you direct your enquiry to the author's publisher.

Yours sincerely

Tania Denning
Strategic Co-ordination Group

ipcmagazines

Our ref:A.003

Michael Gomes
Marketing Manager
McDonalds
DX No: 52051 East Finchley

Dear Mr Gomes

I am Woman's Realm Magazine's official complainer and I write on behalf of one of our readers who has expressed the following concern about your restaurants.

She is a devout fan of the food which you serve in particular the remarkable consistency which you seem to achieve worldwide. It is quite amazing how a Chicken McNugget in London tastes exactly the same as a Chicken McNugget in Melbourne. There is however one inconsistency which you have yet to iron out.

In the grand scheme of McDonalds Chicken McNuggets, McDonalds Fish McNuggets, McDonalds McMuffin, McDonalds Chicken McSandwiches, Mcdonalds McRegular Fries and McDonalds McSmiling Staff, one item sticks out like a sore thumb.

The Big Mac.

Surely it should not bear this name at all. If you were serious about consistency it would not be called The Big Mac. It would be called The Big Mc.

I would be most grateful indeed if you could let me know when this irritating fly in the ointment of McDonalds perfection will finally be expunged.

Yours Mcsincerely

Jasper McGriegson

PS. I hope you will be buying a copy of my new book "The Complainer's Guide to Getting Even". You appear on page 15.

17th November 1994

Mr Griegson
IPC Magazines Limited
King's Reach Tower
Stamford St
London   SE1 9LS

McDonald's Restaurants Ltd

11-59 High Road
East Finchley
London N2 8AW
Telephone 081 883 6400
Facsimile 081 444 5377

Dear Mr Griegson

Thank you for your interesting letter on the Big Mac. I understand your comments, but as you can see from the examples you used in your letter 'Mc' is a pre-fix and does not stand alone as a word.

The Big Mac was invented 26 years ago by a franchisee in Pittsburgh, USA. It had therefore been in existence for six years by the time the first McDonald's restaurant opened in the UK in 1974. It may seem an anomaly, but I can find no certain explanation for its name except perhaps that it was named after one of the two brothers, Mac and Dick McDonald, who operated the first McDonald's restaurant.

You may like to update your mailing list as Mr Gomes has never been the Marketing Manager and actually works in the restaurant side of the business.

Yours sincerely

Veronica Foster
Corporate Communications

LONG AGO, THE McDONALD BROTHERS FINALISE THEIR PLANS:

NAME: McDonalds
FOOD: Burgers, fries, Happy meals
NAME OF BIG BURGER: ?

I JUST DON'T KNOW. 'BIG MAC' OR 'BIG Mc'?

HOW ABOUT 'Bg Mac'?

13 February 1996

Michael O'Leary
Ryan Air
Corporate Head Office
Dublin Airport
County Dublin
Ireland

Dear Mr O'Leary

I am London Newstalk Radio's Official Complainer and I write on behalf of Mr Earl Judge
with whom you have recently had an exchange of correspondence.

As you will see from the attached I have expressed Mr Judge's grievance in a way which I hope
will encourage you to respond sympathetically.

I would be most grateful indeed for your early response.

Yours sincerely

Jasper Griegson

DUBLIN DISASTER

Mr Judge is a very good judge
And so he chose with care
An airline with distinction
And the name of Ryanair.

His destination was Dublin
To spend his Christmas day
He took a bag of clothing
For the time he'd be away.

He checked his bag in
Thinking that
When he arrived
He'd get it back.

But alas it transpired
That due to you
The bag diverted
To Timbuktu.

His trouserless, topless
Yuletide break
Was totally spoiled
By your mistake.

But he couldn't bear
The crudity
Of Christmas
Spent in nudity.

He used his money
Which was no small beer
And bought himself
Some Christmas gear.

I trust the policy
At Ryanair
Is just and kind
And totally fair.

And so I hope
You'll use your might
To sort things out
And put this right.

Corporate Head Office
Dublin Airport
County Dublin
Ireland
Telephone: + *353 1* 844 4400
Telex: 33588 FROP EI
Sita: DUBHQFR

Our Ref: MOL/HMc

19th February 1996

Without Prejudice

Mr Jasper Griegson
c/o The Complainer
London Radio Services Limited
72 Hammersmith Road
London W14 8YE
England

Dear Mr Griegson

I thank you for your interesting letter of the 13th of February last, which I much enjoyed reading. Unfortunately, however, our position has already been clearly set out to Mr Judge in our previous correspondence, and I regret that I can go no further in this case.

Yours sincerely

Michael O'Leary
Chief Executive

27 February 1996

M O'Leary Esq
Ryanair
Dublin Airport
County Dublin
Ireland

Dear Mr O'Leary

Thanks for your letter,
I see you don't care,
I'll make this quite clear,
When I'm next on the the air.

Yours sincerely

Jasper Griegson

David Lloyd Esq
Chairman
David Lloyd Leisure plc
The Arena
Parkway West
Cranford Lane
Hounslow

15th January 1997

Dear David

Re: The Strife of Spice

I write on behalf of a good friend of mine Mrs Kim Rosenfeld.

Kim encountered the most extraordinary problem at your Bushey club at approximately 5pm last Monday. I would be grateful for your comments.

Jamie (Kim's seven year old son) had just finished a swimming lesson. Kim returned to the family changing room to retrieve her son's clothes from a locker and to dress him. On her arrival at the entrance to the room she discovered a no entry sign and a burly assistant blocking her path. She was told that she could not enter because it was not safe.

The reality of the situation was that the room was being used by one of the *Spice Girls* (Geri - the one with the scarlet locks and the armour-plated boobs). Kim was confused. What was so unsafe about the generously endowed red head?

There was no reason to suppose that Geri was carrying some rare but highly contagious tropical disease. There was nothing obvious to suggest that Geri's female accessories were about to explode. In fact there was nothing unsafe at all about entering the room other than the threat seeing Geri in the flesh and discovering that she is nothing more than a silicone blow up doll.

Kim pays in excess of seven hundred pounds each year for family membership of the club and felt aggrieved that she was denied access to the changing room in quite farcical circumstances. What should she have done? She could hardly have left the club in freezing temperatures with her son wet and unclad.

In the end she took the law into her own hands, barged into the room, dried and dressed Jamie.

I would be most grateful indeed for your confirmation that your organisation always keeps as a priority the interests of its *ordinary* members. It seems painfully obvious that on this occasion the *ordinary* members were treated like cattle simply because somebody famous had dropped in for a photo session.

I look forward to hearing from you.

Yours sincerely

J. Grieg

23 January 1997
Ref: SP/jb

DAVID LLOYD LEISURE PLC
THE ARENA,
PARKWAY WEST,
CRANFORD LANE,
HOUNSLOW,
MIDDLESEX TW5 9QA

TELEPHONE: 0181-564 8778
FACSIMILE: 0181-564 9333

Dear Mr Griegson

Thank you for your wonderfully scripted letter dated 15 January 1997 regarding the strife of spice. A thoroughly entertaining letter although containing a very serious point.

We are fortunate enough to attract top personalities to the Bushey Club who are treated with the same respect given to all members. Generally these personalities can visit the club without being noticed. This provides a pleasant visit for both the personality and the remainder of club users.

Unfortunately (or fortunately) the Spice Girls are high profile due to their current success. Almost everybody knows of the Spice Girls. In fact most of them are easily recognisable.

Geri visits the Club as a paying guest of another member and has done previously. Geri's previous visit created shock waves throughout the club. A group gathered outside the ladies changing room and a number of boys aged up to 15 years old attempted to rush into the chaning rooms!

Our course of action on her second visit was to quietly walk Geri through the club and allow her to change in the family changing room, an area which is out of the way. The room was checked firstly by the Duty Manager to see if any lockers were occupied, none were. This action was successful in allowing the club to function as normal and giving Geri a safe haven from the fans. A sign was placed on the door stating that the room was temporarily out of use for the period of her occupancy, no burly assistant was employed. Hence priority was given to the majority of members in an effort for all to use the club as normal.

I am sure you will understand that the intention of the club was to allow normal function rather than the hysteria of her previous visit. Red carpets are rolled out for all members of the club.

Please pass on our apologies for any inconvenience caused to your friend, Mrs Rosenfeld.

Yours sincerely

STEVE PHILPOTT
MANAGING DIRECTOR

London **radio**

a Reuter company

THE COMPLAINER

23 January 1996

D J Sainsbury, Esq
Chairman
J Sainsbury plc
Stamford House
Stamford Street
London, SE1 9LL

Dear Mr Sainsbury

I am London Newstalk Radio's Official Complainer and I write on behalf of our listeners Mrs Tracy Riley.

Last week Tracy sat down ready to tuck into one of your excellent vegetable lasagne ready meals. She enjoys her veg and the sumptuous combination of tomatoes, courgettes and spinach looked enticing. Once cooked, it generated an exotic aroma with overtones of rustic Tuscany. All in all the meal had the hallmarks of a culinary masterpiece.

It was then that disaster struck.

Notwithstanding the bold promise of "suitable for vegetarians" written on the side of the packet, Tracy discovered that the meal contained an unwanted meat element in the form of a rotting dead fly called Herbert.

The good news is that Herbert died replete.

The bad news is that Tracy is disgusted by dead flies in her food and would like (a) a carefully considered response from you (a reply from your "Customer Services Department" will not suffice) and (b) a decent burial for Herbert whose remains, together with the packet are enclosed.

I look forward to hearing from you.

Yours sincerely

Jasper Griegson

David Sainsbury
Chairman & Chief Executive

2nd February 1996

Dear Mrs Riley

I was sorry to learn of your recent experience with one of our Vegetable Lasagne's. Clearly we have let you down in this instance, and I would like to assure you that this matter will be taken up most strongly by the buyer of this product with the supplier concerned.

In light of the disappointment we have caused you, I have taken the liberty of enclosing a voucher which I would like you to use to give us another chance to serve you properly.

In the meantime, many thanks for giving me the opportunity to respond to your complaint.

Yours sincerely

David B...

Our ref: R1/p/0.ff

10 February 1998

Jim Ratcliffe Esq.
Managing Director
Granada Technology Group plc
Granada House
Anthill Road
Bedford NK42 9QQ

Dear Jim

Re: Zappergate

I write on behalf of a friend of mine, Miss Rosalind Wolfe.

Miss Wolfe is deeply distressed at her treatment by your company but I have no doubt that your personal intervention will resolve matters.

For in excess of three years Miss Wolfe has rented a television and video recorder from your shop in the Fulham Road. The remote control for the television has never functioned, does not function now and looks unlikely to function before the year 3000. Miss Wolfe might just as well point a King-size Mars bar at her gogglebox: it would produce no better result. She is zapperless, pure and simple and for a couch potato like her, the effects are potentially devastating.

Miss Wolfe has complained on eight occasions to the shop but to no avail.

I assume that next to your desk is an impressive high tech machine, akin to a remote control, with a large flashing red button, which you can press to rectify consumer complaints such as this.

Please press that button now.

Miss Wolfe and I await with bated breath your earliest reply.

Yours sincerely

J. Grig

Jasper Griegson

Granada Technology
Granada House
Ampthill Road
Bedford MK42 9QQ
Telephone 01234 355233
Facsimile 01234 226090

13 February 1998

Granada Home Technology

Dear Mr Griegson

Thank you for your letter dated 10 February addressed to James Ratcliffe, which has been passed to me for my attention.

I am sorry that you have had to become involved in this regrettable matter but appreciate you bringing this to our attention on behalf of your friend Miss Wolfe.

The matter has been taken in hand and a remote control has been forwarded direct from our service department. I am at a loss as to why this had not previously been actioned but rest assured this will be taken up with those concerned.

Thank you once again for putting pen to paper and for your portrayal of the situation.

Yours sincerely

Sandra Rosborough
<u>Managing Directors Office</u>

SR 03799

7

Prevention is Better Than Cure

There is no doubt that you can achieve success with some complaints before even reaching the starting blocks. As with medicine, prevention is better than cure. If you can spot the tell tale signs you are half way there. The following are the five golden tips to avoiding trauma before ever coming close to encountering it.

1. If it sounds too good to be true, it is too good to be true

Readers of American magazines and newspapers during the 1950s and 60s must have been on hallucinogenic drugs if they believed some of the adverts prevalent at the time. *For a mere $5 you too can become the proud owner of a pair of X-ray glasses. Here's $10, please rush me today my copy of How to Become a 200 pound Muscleman.* What did the creators of these products take the American public for? A bunch of fools? No. To be accurate they took them for (a) a bunch of fools and (b) millions of dollars.

Unfortunately most consumers suffer from an absolutely pathetic form of greed. They think that it is possible to either get something very valuable for tuppence ha'penny or better still for free. If you ever see life insurance advertised with the offer that if you sign up for twenty-five years' worth of cover you will get a 'free' digital alarm clock, don't take the cover, run for cover. As Thomas More might have said, sell your soul to the devil for a Ferrari but not for a digital alarm clock. Even worse than pathetic freebies are goods or services which are so transparently fake that to buy them is to engage in a form of self-delusion close to fantasy. Mortgages offered (in big bold lettering) at 'the never to be repeated' rate of 2 per cent are mortgages with a sting in the tail. Close inspection will reveal that the registered corporate name of the lender is Shark Infestments and that, after a year's worth of borrowing at 2 per cent you will be stung with what the Book of Leviticus calls usury.

2. The small print giveth but the large print taketh away

Everyone knows that the small print is crucial. Insurers (again) are the most common culprits. You may think that because your arm's been lopped off in a moped accident that your five star, supersexy holiday insurance will fly you out of the Greek island of Pistofinos and off to civilisation. Well it won't. You forgot to read clause 13(4)b which states quite categorically that if your accident occurred at a weekend in July then you are absolutely stuffed, or words to that effect. Fortunately there is now some very helpful European legislation on this subject but that won't help you to get your arm sewn back on.

One way to test the importance of the small print is to take a ruler to the large print. If the large print is higher than 1 cm then the large print is 99 per cent manure and the small print is 99 per cent binding legalese drafted by a large firm of expensive London lawyers who will have your butt for breakfast if you challenge it.

3. Never be blinded by science

Many companies who are selling a particularly bad or expensive product or service adhere to the following principle – if you can't beat them confuse them. Miracle cure herbal remedies for example will often be advertised with language so flowery you can virtually smell the scent coming off the page. The reality is that there is an overwhelming wish on the part of the producer to shroud its placebo (masquerading as a panacea) in a verbal fog. In the middle of the haze, the consumer loses his or her way and might not do the crucial thing which is of course to question the efficacy of the item.

4. If it looks like a duck and it talks like a duck and it walks like a duck – it's a duck

All retailers know that consumers are greedy. People will drive many miles to save five pence off a jar of coffee or a litre of petrol. Accordingly, the fantasy factor can creep in again and a consumer can become consumed with greed to the point where he or she becomes totally irrational. If you spot a fifty pound money off coupon in your newspaper, drive ten miles to the superstore concerned, search for the mother of all televisions and then discover that the offer only applies to sets without a remote control, do not buy the wretched thing. Part of your brain will tell you that you are saving fifty pounds and that this is an opportunity not to be missed. The sensible other part will tell you that you are an overweight lazy couch potato who needs a remote control and will hate yourself for expending half a calorie of energy every time you get up to change channels. If it looks like crap, it is crap. Avoid it.

5. The Comeback Principle

On the whole do not buy things from small shops, buy them from large well-known chain stores. The latter will respond to complaints if it all goes horribly wrong in a way which the shop on the corner cannot and will not. It is a cliché to say that you have comeback with a large organisation but it is unfortunately true. Why? For starters, fifty quid means nothing to Tesco, Marks & Spencer or British Airways – it does mean something to the sole trader who runs a shop on the corner. Secondly, megacompanies have to respond in a polite and positive way to serious complaints otherwise they know that, in a metaphorical sense at least, they might find Esther Razen's teeth biting into their shins. Thirdly, the big boys are susceptible to the panoply of Japeresque complaining ploys which have zero effect on a one man band.

In short, when it comes to complaining, big is beautiful.

11th November 1997

Mr Justice Laddie
Royal Courts of Justice
Strand
London WC2

Dear Sir

I read with great interest your judgment delivered last week concerning *Cadbury's Swiss Chalet* chocolate bars.   As I understand the case, you held that chocolate lovers throughout the land are at risk of confusion. You fear, it seems, that the less bright members of the chocolate community might buy the offending confectionary in the mistaken belief that it comes from Switzerland rather than Bournville. I hesitate to criticise what is no doubt an unappealable finding but the problem which exercises my mind is this:-

Where do Mars bars come from?

I await your urgent response.

Yours sincerely

Jasper Griegson

Ms J. Sharman
Chief Executive
Historic Buildings and
Monuments Commission
23 Saville Row
London W1X 1AB

13th March 1996

Dear Ms Sharman

I wish to register a complaint and I would be most grateful indeed for your urgent assistance.

Last week I was standing at Trafalgar Square feeding some pigeons when I made a quite startling discovery. Looking at the Houses of Parliament from the steps of the National Gallery, I realised that Nelson's Column needs to be moved approximately five yards to the east. As you know, the late Lord Nelson gazes straight down Whitehall. The problem is simply that Lord Nelson's line of vision does not achieve its intended objective - it is slightly askew and needs a spot of fine tuning.

In all the circumstances I would be very appreciative if you could rustle up some lottery money or something and ensure that a bit of financial resource is devoted towards this worthy project.

I have carried out some initial financial research and my cash flow diagrams suggest that if we move quickly we could get the column shifted and correctly aligned within a couple of months. In any event I would have thought that this should certainly be sorted out before 2005, the year which will of course be the 200th anniversary of Lord Nelson's famous frog-bashing victory.

I would be most grateful indeed for your comments..

Yours sincerely

Jasper Griegson

ENGLISH HERITAGE

18 March 1997

Dear Mr Griegson

Thank you for your letter dated 13 March 1996 which arrived on 14 March 1997. Mrs Sharman has asked me to reply.

I should point out that the distributor of heritage lottery money is the Heritage Lottery Fund and not English Heritage and that Trafalgar Square is managed by the Department of National Heritage.

However, before you contact either of those organisations, could I suggest you test your ideas for public support and public benefit. You will have to demonstrate both if you are serious about your concerns.

Yours sincerely

Christine Wall

CHRISTINE WALL OBE
Public Affairs Director

John Oates
Joint Managing Director
Marks & Spencer plc
Michael House
Baker Street
London W1A 1DN

15th February 1997

Dear John

Re: The Mysterious Case of James-Daman Willems

I write on behalf a good friend of mine Mrs TJ Riley who encoun-
-tered an extraordinary problem with your store in Uxbridge.

In November last year Mrs Riley (a devoted fan of M & S) decided to buy some shorts for her son. She went to Uxbridge (wasted trip number one) only to discover that there were a number of problems in doing this which I won't bore you with. The shorts had to be ordered from your warehouse. When the shorts finally arrived Mrs Riley returned to Uxbridge (wasted trip number two) only to find, when she got home, that the contained a label bearing the name James-Daman Willems! She returned the shorts (wasted trip number three) and obtained a refund.

Mrs Riley's only gripe is that she wasted three hours of her life and her only compensation was a cold-hearted apology for any inconvenience caused. During this time span she could have watched two games of football, driven to Manchester, visited a museum or started to construct a box girder bridge. You can't give Mrs Riley three hours back but you can demonstrate that M & S is a company which genuinely wants to foster goodwill with its customers. Please restore her faith in the notion of good customer relations.

I enclose a copy of her receipt and the offending label.

Yours sincerely

J. Griey

Jasper Griegson

MARKS & SPENCER

REGISTERED OFFICE: MICHAEL HOUSE · BAKER STREET · LONDON WIA IDN
FACSIMILE: 0171-487 2679 · CABLES: MARSPENZA LONDON · TELEX: 267141
TELEPHONE: 0171-935 4422

26 February 1997

Our Ref: JOY/1543949/002/TP

Dear Mr Griegson

Thank you for your letter dated 22 February.

From your original correspondence, I was unaware that you were referring to the letter sent from this office in December and I had presumed that you were referring to our store's handling of Mrs Riley's complaint. Therefore, please accept my apologies for any further concern my response has caused.

I do appreciate Mrs Riley's concern and the inconvenience she experienced, and I am enclosing a gift voucher for £25.00 for you to pass on to your friend, as a gesture of goodwill.

Thank you for writing.

Yours sincerely

J. Edmonds

MISS JOY EDMONDS
Customer Adviser
0171-268 1234

7 May 1997

Mr J Griegson
c/o Jeremy Robson
Robson Books Ltd
Bolsover House
Clipstone Street
London W1

Dear Mr Griegson

On a particularly cold and dreary Saturday last January, having nothing better to do, I went to my local library. Most unfortunately, as it turned out, your book entitled "The Professional Complainer's Guide to Getting Even" caught my eye and I borrowed it and took it home.

I spent the afternoon reading aloud from it to my son. It was so extraordinarily amusing that for quite a considerable time I was completely helpless with laughter. Like many people I had not had much to laugh about for several years and the unaccustomed exercise was too much for my neck and throat muscles which were severely sprained. As a result of this I had to spend the rest of the weekend with a hot water bottle clutched to the affected areas.

I am therefore claiming the following:

- Damages for pain and suffering

- The cost of the hot water

I have not claimed for the wear and tear on the hot water bottle as I was able to get a full refund from the vendor (J Sainsbury) when it developed a leak a few days later

It also occurs to me that the few hours of pure enjoyment your book gave me will have prolonged my life, perhaps by as much as a week - another week of expense, rheumatism, and unruly grandchildren - so I require compensation for that too.

I await your proposals.

Yours sincerely

Ceira Ennis

Mrs C M Ennis

19th May 1997

Dear Mrs Ennis

Thank you for your letter of 7 May.

What can I say? We appear to be heading intractably towards expensive and acrimonious High Court litigation. The only way to avert such a calamitous collision-course is for:-

☺   You to send me five packets of chocolate buttons together with an apology or

☺   You to send me twenty large bars of *Cadbury's Dairy Milk* together with an apology published in *The Times* or

☺   You to send me my bodyweight in Godiva hand-made champagne truffles whilst you douse yourself in petrol and light a match as a supreme token of your remorse.

You weren't suggesting that I should compensate you were you?

Yours sincerely

J. Grig

Jasper Griegson

Our ref:mor.TAL1ty

27th July 1987

The Man in Charge
The Highways Department
London Borough of Hillingdon
Civic Centre
Uxbridge UB8 1UW

Dear Sir

As as ratepayer and motorist in your borough, I wish to register a complaint about the dreadful state of the road surface on Maxwell Road.

It is so full of holes that is more reminiscent of a lunar landscape than a leafy suburban street. Since I do not possess either a moon-buggy, a Sherman tank or radar I would be most grateful for written confirmation from you that if any damage is done to my car, you will be financially responsible. Unless I hear from you within 24 Earth hours I will assume that this arrangement is acceptable.

Yours sincerely

J. Grieg

Jasper Griegson

London Borough of Hillingdon

Central Depot Harlington Road, Hillingdon, Middlesex, UB8 3EY

UXBRIDGE 51188

Please reply to: The Director of Engineering

Your Ref:

My Ref: SL/JA

Enquiries to Mr S. Pilgrim ext 262

Date 5th August 1987

Dear Sir,

Thank you for your letter dated the 27th July 1987 regarding the carriageway surface at Maxwell Road in Northwood.

Due to the construction of a Supermarket by Costain, improvements are being made to the junction of Maxwell Road and Green Lane. When these have been completed this area will be resurfaced. During the construction period we will monitor the situation and undertake temporary repairs as necessary.

Yours faithfully,

S. PILGRIM
ASSISTANT ENGINEER

16th August 1987

S. Pilgrim Esq
The Highways Department
London Borough of Hillingdon
Central Depot
Harlington Road
Hillingdon
Middx
UB8 3EY

Dear Mr Pilgrim

Please let me know what progress you are making!

Yours sincerely

Jasper Griegson

8

Ten Reasons Why Complaining is Better Than Sex

For the unenlightened, a wrestling match with a member of the opposite gender is the supreme *joie de vivre*. This view of life is misconceived, misguided and pretty boring. Complaining is the most fulfilling activity which any human being can perform. A comparison with sex bears this out. A week after posting your moaning missive, the sound of the postman's feet trudging towards your front door with a white envelope is the kind of tantalising foreplay that will, after a while, send a tingle down your spine. The arrival of the letter through your letter-box is the conjugal act which culminates in the excitement which you can only experience by ripping open the envelope. The realisation that the letter bears a personally penned apology from the Chairman of a multinational company and encloses a fat compensatory cheque is the pinnacle of pleasure. Trust me. Try it.

The following comparison between these two activities illustrates the point.

1   Complaining is unlikely to produce an end product

which cries in the middle of the night, engages in projectile vomiting without warning and grows up to hate you because you drive a Ford Mondeo and like classical music.

2   Complaining when you are over forty will not do your back in. On the contrary, it will relieve the very stresses and strains which beset menopausal women and mid-life-crisis-stricken men.

3   You can complain any time of the night or day and can even do so in a public place if you feel the sudden urge. If you complain together with your partner on the fourth floor of Marks & Spencer in Oxford Street you will not be arrested.

4   You need not feel guilty if you complain without passion. Complaining can be sparked off by and carried out with a whole gamut of emotions ranging from hatred to lust. You will not need therapy if you complain badly.

5   You don't have to form a lasting relationship when you complain to someone. A one off complaint to the Managing Director of Currys can be satisfying, pleasurable and, if executed properly, can leave you with a nice warm glowing feeling at the end of the experience.

6   If you complain for a living you will not be shunned by ordinary people or telephoned by Conservative MPs enquiring about French lessons.

7   Complaining is safe. When putting a letter in an envelope and shoving the envelope in a post-box you do not need protection. Even if you repeat the exercise ten times a week for years on end it is very unlikely to bring you out in an embarrassing, socially-unacceptable rash.

8   Even if you are a kinky complainer you will rarely

have to splash out on expensive sado-masochistic instruments of torture. Occasionally you may feel a profound desire to express yourself by chaining your limbs to the railings outside the head office of Woolworths but this is about as bizarre as complaining gets.

9   If you are a hideously ugly dwarf with the sex appeal of a wilted lettuce your performance as a complainer will not be restricted. On one occasion I photocopied my repulsive mush and attached it to my letter of complaint with devastatingly positive results. This kind of tactic tends not to produce the same degree of success if the objective is to lure a member of the opposite sex into a lasting and meaningful relationship.

10   Being sexy is expensive. By the time you have purchased the latest Lagerfeld aftershave, a smart new shirt, a bunch of roses and the price of a candle-lit dinner, its just about time to remortgage your house. A letter of complaint on the other hand costs 26 pence.

24 January 1995

Tim Daniels Esq
Managing Director
Selfridges
Oxford Street
London
W1A 1AB

Dear Mr Daniels

<u>KNOB</u>

I wish to register a complaint of the most serious kind.

For many eons I have been a great fan of your store. This faith was sadly shattered when I spent £220 on a Gaggia cappuccino machine on 5 January 1995. In short, the knob has dropped off as a result of a defective spring. In all the circumstances, there is only one way for this to be rectified and that is for you to supply me with a new knob as soon as possible. Unless I receive the same within three working days, I intend to commit suicide by putting the steamer pipe from the cappuccino machine (if I can make it work) into my mouth.

I await your urgent response.

Yours sincerely

<u>Jasper Griegson</u>

SELFRIDGES

25 January 1995

Dear Mr Griegson

KNOB

Don't do it!

Your letter addressed to Tim Daniels has been passed to me for attention as the Cook Shop falls within my area of responsibility. As you might imagine I now feel personally accountable for your serious complaint and concerned for your continued good health!!

We do take Customer Care extremely seriously and I just hope that we can meet the three day deadline which you set. My Cook Shop Buyer, Amanda Newey has despatched a replacement knob under separate cover, accompanied by a complimentary pack of Doewe Egberts coffee, which I trust will help ease the trauma?

Please let me know when you have the Cappuccino machine working satisfactorily again as I am going to worry about this for the rest of the week.

In the meantime, thank you quite seriously for your letter and for bringing a touch of humour into our pressured existence.

Yours sincerely

Rob Green
Merchandise Director

cc: Tim Daniels
    Amanda Newey / Gill Osborne

ipcmagazines

Realm

20 February 1995

Debbie Machugh
General Manager
Jeffrey Rogers
184-192 Drummond Street
London, NW1 3HP

Dear Ms Machugh

I am Woman's Realm Magazine's Official Complainer and I write on behalf of Ms Sigal Joory whose letter to me is attached for ease of reference.

Ms Joory is gutted. She parted company with 35 smackeroos in exchange for which she has received the following: not a sausage. She thought that she was getting a suit. What in fact she got was a piece of material which is so see through it might just as well be made of cellophane. This was not apparent in the half light of your dingy changing rooms. As soon as Ms Joory tried it on at home (with appropriate comments from all around her) the harsh reality soon became crystal clear.

Given that Ms Joory is attempting to advance her career in the second oldest profession rather than the oldest profession she feels that less transparent clothing would probably be more appropriate for a female City executive. I enclose the garment for your laboratory analysis and I look forward to receiving (a) a refund; (b) a large box of chocolates; and/or (c) a report on my desk explaining the position. Unless Ms Joory hears from you with a positive response she will have no option but to parade her wares in the said garment at your Whiteleys branch in the course of next week. I look forward to hearing from you.

Best wishes.

Yours sincerely

Jasper Griegson

February 23rd 1995

Dear Miss Joory,

In reference to the enclosed letter from Mr Jasper Griegson I express my apologies to you for the fact that you had to complain via a third party therefore delaying an outcome.

Obviously as the skirt is unlined it will be, in certain angles, see-through. I am therefore happy to have the skirt lined for you, making it more suitable for the purpose for which it was purchased. If however this is not acceptable because you have simply changed your mind, I will in this instance make an exception and refund the outfit.

I look forward to hearing from you so I can deal with this matter promptly.

Yours sincerely,

Debbie McHugh
(Area Manager)

On behalf of Jeffrey Rogers Retail Ltd

JEFFREY ROGERS plc

133

Sir Richard Greenbury
Marks & Spencer
Michael House
Baker Street
London W1

18 October 1994

Dear Sir Richard

As you know, I am Womans Realm Magazine's official complainer and I write on behalf of Ms R del Tufo.

Ms del Tufo is the proud owner of the enclosed blue suede shoe which she purchased from your Oxford Circus store for the princely sum of £25. Ms del Tufo's problems are twofold:

1.   The blue suede shoes which she hoped would transform her into something more attractive proved to be glossy, worn out hooves within a couple of weeks (as no doubt your laboratory analysis will show).

2.   Ms del Tufo has been looking for a prince for some time and given the peculiar shape of her feet has had some difficulty in finding the silver slipper which might produce the man of her dreams. She hoped that one of your blue suede shoes would do the trick. Obviously she has been mistaken.

In all the circumstances I would be most grateful indeed if you could restore Ms del Tufo's faith in your company and the quality of its products. At the very least you could save her having to kiss a lot of frogs (or am I getting my fairy stories mixed up?).

Best regards.

Yours sincerelv

Jasper Griegson

MARKS & SPENCER

REGISTERED OFFICE: MICHAEL HOUSE · BAKER STREET · LONDON W1A 1DN
FACSIMILE: 071-487 2679 · CABLES: MARSPENZA LONDON · TELEX: 267141
TELEPHONE: 071-935 4422

Mr J Greigson
Realm Ipc Magazines Ltd
King'S Reach Tower
Stamford Street
SE1 9LS

01 November 1994

Our Ref: ESF/1179263/001/TC

Dear Mr Greigson

Thank you for your letter addressed to the Chairman. As a member of the Corporate Affairs Group, I have been asked to investigate the matter on his behalf.

I am sorry to learn of Ms Del Tufo's problems with a pair of shoes she has purchased from this Company. I do hope you will offer her our sincere apologies for all the concern and inconvenience this has caused.

We have now had the opportunity of having the shoes examined by our technical expert in the relevant department. You may be interested to learn his comments following that examination.

Firstly, the shoes are made from a material called 'Nubuck', which has a silky surface. In order to maintain and preserve this finish it is necessary to brush the shoes regularly with a soft nylon brush.

Secondly, in using this soft material, the shoe upper was intentionally designed to be unstructured, and the sole flexible and absorbing in order to provide comfort during wear. I regret that Ms Del Tufo found that this was not the case.

In view of this, I am enclosing gift vouchers to the value of £40.00 in order for her to select a suitable alternative.

Thank you again for bringing this to our attention.

Yours sincerely,

Elaine Fuller

MRS ELAINE FULLER

17 November 1995

S Knibbs, Esq
Managing Director
UCI United Cinemas International
90 Great Bridge
Water Street
Manchester, M1 5JW

Dear Mr Knibbs

Re: Extraterrestrial Calamity

I wish to register a complaint.

26 October is my birthday. My wife decided this year that as a treat we would visit the UCI Cinema at Leicester Square to see the film Apollo 13. We paid in advance by telephone credit card booking and I took the afternoon off work. We arrived at the cinema only to be told by an official well versed in the language of Shakespeare and Chaucer that:-

"Sorry Guv, the Cinema's shut. Her 'Ighness Princess Diana is coming".

At this point and very much in tone with the dialogue of the film which we were hoping to watch, my wife said to me:-

"We have a problem".

The nub of the problem was that there was a Royal Premier that night and the person who had taken our telephone booking had made a mistake. Needless to say my birthday treat was ruined.

I would be most grateful indeed if you would zoom into action and investigate this unhappy saga. I look to you personally for a meaningful and positive response.

Yours sincerely

Jasper Griegson

21 November 1996

Dear Mr Griegson

From the experience you outline I fully appreciate any dissatisfaction you feel with the advanced booking service of the Central Box Office. The poor performance you received undoubtedly falls short in our aim to professionally and correct meet customer requirements. Therefore please be assured further investigation will be made into the matter.

However, there seems to be some confusion surrounding your booking. As you can see from the transaction details, the book was made on the 25th October for the *27th* October. I can only surmise at this stage that the Operator who dealt with your booking either misinterpreted or misheard your request, or was not fully conversed with the happenings of UCI Empire at that time.

Please accept my apologies for the compounded consequences and considerable inconveniences caused to you by this booking error.

I can confirm that your account has been recredited by the cinema to the amount of £12.00, and in addition hope that the enclosed Guest Pass provides some recompense to the disappointment you must have felt. The pass admits two people and can be redeemed at the cinema anytime before the end of February 1997, except when the Free List is suspended. For further details please contact the Cinema Box Office.

With these I trust that your next visit to UCI Empire is more successful and enjoyable.

Yours sincerely

Alice Uren
Central Box Office - Customer Services Department

Sir Terence Conran
22 Shad Thames
London
SE1 2YU

18th August 1997

Dear Sir Terence

I wish to make a complaint.

My wife's a thirsty old bird and late on the afternoon of Wednesday 13th August she and her mate dropped into your watering hole at Le Pont de la Tour. They only fancied a couple of bevvies which, to be perfectly frank, they knocked back in no time.

After having tanked up, my wife asked for the bill which she paid for with what was admittedly a pretty ropy looking twenty pound note. This caused a problem. The bill came to Pds 19-49

inclusive of service.

She was kept waiting for her 51 pence change for ten minutes but nevertheless held on. The waiter in question was obviously loath to cough up and was determined to make my wife suffer despite the fact that she had paid in full

inclusive of service.

Eventually the waiter slammed the 51 pence down with bad grace making his contempt both visible and audible to the surrounding customers.

You personally were in the restaurant being photographed at the time but wife didn't have the bottle to involve you. I would now like to do precisely that.

Do you think that the words

inclusive of service

mean just what they say or not? I would welcome your view. I have both noshed and boozed at a number of your eateries including Mezzo, Café Bluebird and Quaglino's but I have never encountered this kind of hostility before.

I await your comments.

Yours sincerely

J. Griey

Jasper Griegson

LE PONT DE LA TOUR

ON THE RIVER BY TOWER BRIDGE

Dear Mr Griegson   26nd August 1997

Following your letter to Sir Terence Conran which he passed to me as I am the General Manager of the Gastrodrome.

Please accept my apologies for the inconvenience caused to your wife and her guest on Wednesday 13th August. I have spoken to the Manager and can ensure you that our intention is to provide the best service at all times, even if it is a busy day.

Our objective is to look after our customers in the best possible way, I am sorry if your wife thought we had failed to do so on this occasion, but please be assured that the situation has been discussed with our staff (Please find attached a cheque for the full refund of £19.49).

I hope this incident will not deter you from coming back to Le Pont de la Tour as we certainly value our customers.

Yours sincerely

Rémy Lysé
General Manager

cc.   **Sir Terence Conran**

"WAITER THERE'S A SPOON IN MY SOUP!"

9

The Great British Holiday

Every year the Great British Public goes on holiday. There are two kinds of Great British Holiday: bloody awful ones and ones which are an unmitigated total and absolute disaster. For starters the British don't know how to enjoy themselves. Furthermore, most holidaymakers are treated like a lower form of pond life by those who are supposed to be providing a quality service. Many holidays, even those that are 'packaged', have moved on from the breathtakingly appalling 1970s but do not be fooled, all tourists become con-victims at some stage in the process.

I have more than once been accused of going out of my way to look for complaints, especially on holiday. The following poignant story illustrates why I do not need to do this. Down on the north coast of Cornwall near Newquay is a wonderful hotel which will remain nameless unless they decide to pay me some dosh as an advertising fee. My family and I have been there more than once and have never had cause to complain. During our last visit however I was contacted by the BBC to do an early morning stint on Radio 5 talking about complaining of course. When I informed the Hotel Manager that I was broadcasting live the following day and needed a quiet room away from my kids, she asked what the subject-matter was. On being told, she duly obliged by providing me with her office for as long as I needed it! The following day I woke early only to discover, with twenty minutes to go, that the hotel's telephone system had broken down as a result of an electric storm during the night. I made it to a telephone box with seconds to spare and recounted on air how my hotel had been struck by lightning. 'These kind of things happen to you, don't they Jasper?' asked the radio presenter.

Assuming that you are determined to have a really rotten holiday, where should you go?

Spain

Whereas some tourist traps have become more subtle in their dreadfulness, parts of Spain remain as unpalatable as ever. There are some lovely areas but no one goes there. Even bits of the Costa del Sol and Majorca have improved recently but not by design – it is simply that the high alumina cement construction of half the hotels has, quite literally, dissolved. Although the Spaniards are starting to realise that there are regions to be exploited over and above those currently occupied by the Supporters Club of Millwall FC, many of the facilities remain fossilised in time. 1974 to be precise. The 'English Pub' on the outskirts of Palma is still fitted out in garish brown and orange gloss, the male bar staff look like extras from a cheap porn movie and there are few nights when the dulcet tones of 'Tie a Yellow Ribbon' cannot be heard through the loudspeaker system. The funny thing is that these places are so deliciously abominable that they are starting to become museum pieces. When I last went to Spain I couldn't resist a brief visit to some of the lowest proletarian hell-holes.

Eurodisney

There are two parts of France which, unknown to the French, are not part of France at all.

The first is a small island off the coast of Normandy called GCSE France. On this little known atoll the natives speak a special dialect called GCSE French which comprises a motley array of badly pronounced irregular verbs, a vocabulary restricted to the weather and a dictionary called *The Bluffer's Guide to Busking Your Way Through a French Exam*.

The second is a place called Disneyland Paris. It used to be called Eurodisney and it was appalling. The powers that be at this Mickey Mouse organisation decided that in order to improve things all they needed to do was change the name. Funnily enough this had no effect whatsoever. Eurodisney (as I still call it) remains the hideous, wrongly-sited, overpriced American carbuncle that it was on day one. Don't go there.

America

If you are thin, horribly thin, go to America. An anorexic waif need go no further than the airport in search of an immediate solution to thinness. Within a week, the most determined, heath-conscious tourist will have consumed a shed load of waffles with syrup and cream, a stack of multiple-decker Scooby Doo style hamburgers and a pile of chocolate brownies. I like food and therefore I like America. Enough said. After (a) returning and (b) stepping on my scales I will however inevitably say that America is a terrible place and vow never to return. Masochistically, I always do.

Scandinavia

Norway and Sweden are excellent holiday destinations, provided that you are incurably suicidal. The leaden-skies, the steep drops, the incomprehensible humourless monotone of the natives and the price of the beer all combine wonderfully to create an atmosphere which only lemmings know how to enjoy properly. If you are really depressed, book a trip in February, draft a suitable final note and make your way to a drab suburb of Oslo. You may not have been aware of this but Stockholm narrowly defeated Deptford to secure the much coveted poll position in 1997 Golden Suicide Spot Awards. If you are cheerful and do not understand the attraction of living in darkness for long periods of time avoid Scandinavia.

Germany

There is nothing wrong or unpatriotic about flying over Germany. On no account, however, should you attempt to land.

England

The only bit of England worth going to for a holiday is the Lake District. In August 1976 it did not rain there. At all other times it does.

If you are absolutely hell-bent on an apocalyptic mission of misery you need look no further than an English seaside town. Whether it is Blackpool, Morecambe or Frinton you will, even at the fag end of the twentieth century, encounter the following mind-bogglingly awful things:

☹ The smell of rancid fried toast

☹ Games arcades hosted by paedophiles

☹ 'Humorous' saucy postcards bearing 'jokes' composed by Bernard Manning

☹ Rancid fried toast itself and

☹ Guest Houses which can best be described as pretty similar to the residence where 'Mother' lived in the film Psycho.

ipcmagazines

S. Richway Esq.
Managing Director
Virgin Atlantic Airways plc
7th Floor
Sussex House
High Street
Crawley West Sussex
H10 1BZ

7th August 1994

Realm

THE COMPLAINER

Dear Mr Richway

Re: Flight V5012 Boston to Gatwick Sunday 31st July 1994

I am Woman's Realm Magazine's Official Complainer and I write on behalf of one of our most avid readers, Miss Caroline Day

When you fly Virgin Airways Mr Richway I assume that you do not wait in line with what one might unkindly term "the Cattle". I assume (although you may correct me) that you are whisked through the check-out like a hot knife through butter.

Miss Day was not so fortunate with her above-mentioned return flight from Boston.

Miss Day encountered delay and ineptitude of epoch-making proportions. What is surprising is that she was not even travelling Cattle Class but booked through US Airtours "Preference Club".

The problem in essence was this. She arrived at the check-in desk at 7pm for the flight which was due to leave at 8.20pm. Notwithstanding that there were at least 100 people in the queue Miss Day was told to wait in line. For 45 minutes the queue did not move. When it did move it crept along at snail's pace, not least of all because the few check-in staff at hand diminished in number when several of them apparently buggered off for a coffee break.

At 8.10pm the flight was boarding whilst Miss Day was still in line and by now steam was starting to pour out of her ears (see picture below).

When she finally checked in Miss Day was told that she had done so too late and that her seat had been given away. She had booked through USAirtours Preference Club to avoid just this kind of farce.

Miss Day is human not bovine and resents having been treated like a cow ready for the knackers yard.

I would be most grateful indeed if you would take some swift and decisive action to restore Miss Day's faith in your company. Go ahead Mr Richway. Make my day. Make Miss Day's day too.

Yours sincerely

J. Griey

Jasper Griegson

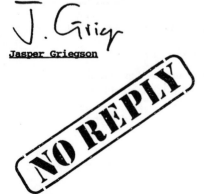

Miss
C. Day
at 8.10pm
on 31/7/94

ipcmagazines

15 November 1994

J. Birt Esq.
Director-General
British Broadcasting Corporation
Television Centre
Wood Lane
London
W12 7RJ

Dear Mr. Birt

I am Women's Realm magazine's Official Complainer and I write on behalf
of one of our readers, Mrs. B. Zietman, who has the following problem.

She is and was a great fan of the Goodies. A month or so ago she heard a
rumour that two videos of some old Goodies shows were allegedly available
in the shops. She then began what appears to have been a fruitless quest
to find them. Having scoured two thousand video shops from W H Smith
in Pinner High Street to an obscure outpost on the planet Pluto, her search
has produced the following results i) Nothing and ii) Nothing and iii)
Nothing.

Mrs Zietman has three theories about the lost videos and I would be
grateful if you could let me know which is correct:

1)   In Bolshevik revolutionary-style the BBC's agents arranged for the
      Goodies to be murdered and their bodies, together with all known
      recordings of their work, have been buried under your patio.

2)   Now in their sad twilight years, the Goodies have retreated to a
      secret location in the Black Forest where they have stockpiled the
      last remaining footage of their antics which they watch day in, day
      out in a painless attempt to bring about their early demise through
      boredom.

3)   The BBC has, in its inimitable, half-hearted, lukewarm style, failed
      to promote what are in fact excellent videos.

I look forward to hearing from you as to what is going on. Please make it
snappy, however – Mrs. Zietman is considering committing suicide using a
lethal oversized black pudding.

Yours sincerely

Jasper Griegson

FROM ADVISER TO THE DIRECTOR-GENERAL
DAVID HATCH CBE

BRITISH BROADCASTING CORPORATION
BROADCASTING HOUSE
LONDON W1A 1AA
TELEPHONE: 071-580 4468
TELEX: 265781
Direct Tel No: 071-765 5005
Direct Fax No: 071-765 5092

18 November 1994

Dear Mr Griegson

Not actually my patch, the chap you want is Nicholas Chapman, the Managing Director of BBC Worldwide Publishing, to whom I've passed your letter.

Of your three theories, I plump for No 2. They're very old now and want to remember their youth. It's not actually the Black Forest but the Black Horse in Cricklewood.

I can't recommend the black pudding suicide method - what's your fetish about all things black? My recommendation would Mr Blobby jelly!

Yours hysterically

David Hatch

Jasper Griegson Esq
Official Complainer
Women's Realm Magazine
Editorial Department
King's Reach Tower
Stamford Street
London SE1 9LS

19TH APRIL 1997

DR N. B. SMITH
CHAIRMAN
BAA PLC
130 WILTON ROAD
LONDON SW1V 1LQ

DEAR DR SMITH

RE: HEATHROW AIRPORT TERMINAL 3 CATASTROPHE

I WISH TO REGISTER A COMPLAINT ON BEHALF OF MY TWO DAUGHTERS, NINA AND ZOE, AGED SEVEN AND FOUR RESPECTIVELY.

A COUPLE OF WEEKS AGO MY FAMILY AND I WERE WAITING AT TERMINAL 3 PENDING THE CALL TO BOARD A SEVEN HOUR FLIGHT TO THE WEST INDIES. UNFORTUNATELY WE WERE NOT FLYING WITH THE EVER-RESOURCEFUL BRITISH AIRWAYS AND IT DAWNED UPON US THAT OUR CHILDREN WERE UNLIKELY TO BE GIVEN ANYTHING IN THE FORM OF ENTERTAINMENT ON THE AEROPLANE. WE DECIDED THAT SOME COLOURED CRAYONS AND SCRIBBLING PADS WERE ESSENTIAL. TO OUR ASTONISHMENT AND IN THE ABSENCE OF A BRANCH OF WH SMITH THERE WERE NO SUCH ITEMS TO BE HAD ANYWHERE IN THE TERMINAL.

ALTHOUGH THE NATURE COMPANY SELLS SOME PROPER ARTISTIC PASTELS FOR ADULTS COSTING ABOUT TEN POUNDS THESE WERE OBVIOUSLY INAPPROPRIATE.

IF YOU HAVE CHILDREN YOU WILL DOUBTLESS APPRECIATE THE DILEMMA WHICH WE FACED. IN THE END WE HAD TO MAKE DO WITH A BLUE PEN AND SOME PLAIN PAPER. I ENCLOSE FOR YOUR URGENT ATTENTION AN EXAMPLE OF THE MINIMALIST ARTWORK WHICH ZOE CREATED WITH THE LIMITED RESOURCES AVAILABLE. I'M SURE YOU'LL AGREE IT'S NOT BAD BUT THE QUESTION WHICH EXERCISES MY MIND IS THIS:

WOULD VAN GOGH'S SUNFLOWERS HAVE LOOKED ANY GOOD IN BIRO?

I AWAIT YOUR COMMENTS.

YOURS SINCERELY

JASPER GRIEGSON

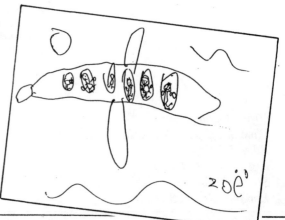

Corporate Office
130 Wilton Road
London SW1V 1LQ

Telephone Switchboard 0171-834 9449
Direct Line 0171-932 6600
Direct Facsimile 0171-932 6603

From the Chairman
Dr N Brian Smith CBE

BAA ◢◤

24 April 1997

Dear Mr. Gregson,

I am writing further to my secretary's letter of 22 April.
I have been in contact with my retail team at Heathrow
Terminal 3 who apologise for the poor range of drawing materials
available in our T3 shops for our younger customers. They have
instructed Alpha Retail who operate the main newsagents to
source and keep in stock the type of products you requested.

However, despite the constraints I am most impressed with Zoe's
aeroplane drawing! I am sure Van Gogh would have been very
complimentary.

As a small gesture of our thanks for bringing this to our
attention, I have asked Danny Sloan, our Acting Retail Director
at Heathrow, to send two sets of drawing materials for Zoe and
Nina to encourage further their artistic talents!

Yours sincerely

Brian Smith

10 June 1997

Terry Leahy
Managing Director
Tesco Stores Plc
Delamere Road
Waltham Cross
London

Dear Mr Leahy

I am a vegetarian and a monkey.

It therefore follows as a matter of axiomatic logic that I like to indulge in bananas. I enclose for your attention what appear to be examples of Tesco's finest. As you will see, however, one of these bananas is more than just a fruit. It appears to be the home to an animal. Given my anti-carnivore inclinations, I am less than happy to discover such a high meat content in what, on any view, would normally be regarded as a non-meat product.

Doubtless, your lab boys will do the 'biz' and in those circumstances, I look forward to hearing from you.

Yours sincerely

Jasper Griegson

Encs

Our Ref: 499534

8 July 1997

Tesco House,
Delamare Road,
Cheshunt,
Hertfordshire EN8 9SL
Telephone: 01992 632222
Facsimile: 01992 644961

Dear Mr Griegson

Further to my letter dated 19 June. Firstly may I apologise for the delay in getting back to you. I have, however, now received the report concerning your bananas.

The specimen was described as a silk encased foreign body. This has subsequently been examined by an entomologist who reports as follows:
"The specimen was identified as the remains of a pupa and cocoon of the moth species *Antichloris* (no common name). This is a harmless tropical moth whose larvae feed on the leaves of the banana palm. The occurrence of these on imported bananas is reasonably commonplace."

Ensuring both the safety and quality of the food we sell is central to our business. All of our bananas are rigorously inspected and the majority are thoroughly washed before we pack them. However, a proportion of our bananas come from plantations in the tropics, where washing facilities are not widely available. We are however continuing to work with such suppliers, to extend the use of these facilities.

We are certain that we take all possible steps to prevent this problem occurring. However, we have had discussions about this type of complaint with the Ministry Of Agriculture, Fisheries And Food who have noted our concerns.

Although it is rare to receive a complaint of this kind, I have told our technologist, who will make sure it is fully investigated. As a gesture of goodwill, I enclose Tesco vouchers to the value of £15.00.

Thank you for allowing me the time to investigate this matter. I do hope that despite this unfortunate incident you will continue to shop at Tesco and be completely satisfied with all future purchases.

Yours sincerely
For and on behalf of Tesco Stores Ltd

Frances Hickling
Customer Service Executive to the Board

28 February 1997

Our Ref : A/lieN

Mrs Anne Brown
Consumer Complaints
Trebor Bassetts Ltd
Maidstone
ME16 0SP

Dear Mrs Brown

I wish to register a complaint of the most serious kind.

I recently became the proud owner of a packet of Maynards Wine Gums. When I opened the packet the first thing I saw was a Wine Gum so hideously deformed that I can only assume that it must have been subjected to a near lethal dose of radiation in the course of its gestation. As you will see, it bears a white discolouring which I imagine is the symptom of some virulent mutation of the bubonic plague. If I were you, I would don some rubber gloves and hand the offending article to your laboratory in a hermetically sealed body bag. On the assumption that you have not died as a result of receiving the enclosure to this letter, I assume that you (or if you have died, your executors) will let me know that the sweet has been jettisoned into outer space - probably the only safe place for alien objects as dangerous as this.

I await your urgent reply.

Yours sincerely

J. Griy

Jasper Griegson

TREBOR BASSETT LTD

KREEMY WORKS
ST PETER STREET MAIDSTONE
KENT ME16 0SP

TELEPHONE 01622 757421
FACSIMILE 01622 688683

AB/1997/03/316   11th March, 1997

Dear Mr. Griegson,

Thank you for your letter concerning the Wine Gums.
We sincerely apologise for the unsatisfactory condition of the
sweet and for the inconvenience this has caused you.

The sample you returned has been examined and found to be starch.
A tray of starch is used to print the shape of the sweets and a
hot cooked syrup is then deposited into these impressions. When
the sweets have set, they are separated from the starch. In this
instance a portion of starch has been wet and has been picked up
on the surface of the sweet.

As you can imagine, we make every effort to maintain high
standards in our factories and depots to ensure that our products
are in first class condition. We are sorry that it was not up
to the quality you expected, and we would like to thank you for
returning the item to us for investigation. We are referring the
matter to our Quality Assurance management in the manufacturing
area concerned.

Please accept our apologies to you for this occurrence in this
instance and hope that the parcel we are forwarding to you will
serve to restore your confidence in the high quality of our
products.

Yours sincerely,

Ann Brown
Consumer Relations Officer.

ipcmagazines

Our ref:1.014

2nd August 1994

The Chairman
Railtrack
40 Bernard Street
London
WC1N 1BY

Dear Sir

I am Woman's Realm Magazine's Official Complainer and I write on behalf of four of our most avid readers who work in an office in Richmond.

For several weeks now they have had dreadful trouble in getting to work as a result the non-existent train service on Wednesdays (and now half day Tuesdays and Thursdays). Having paid several thousand pounds in total for their various season tickets "the Richmond Four" feel hard done by. They say it seems a bit like putting twenty pound notes into a shredding machine.

Unless you resume normal services within the coming week one of the four (Paul) has threatened to protest by tying himself to Blackfriars bridge wearing nothing but a bowler hat and a smile. In order to avoid this hideous display I would be grateful if you would either pay the signalmen or operate the signals yourself. Paul will give you a hand if you like.

I await your earliest reply. In the meantime I would like to take this opportunity to apologise for any inconvenience which this letter may have caused you.

Yours faithfully

Jasper Griegson

RAILTRACK
Robert B Horton *Chairman*

10 August 1994

Re: Readers' Complaint - RMT Signalling Dispute

I deeply regret the RMT's strike action and the frustration it has caused to your four correspondents from Richmond. The continuing action by the RMT is a matter of utmost concern to Railtrack and I and my colleagues are working hard to resolve the dispute.

We are seeking to persuade the RMT to return to the negotiating table to discuss a deal that will reward our signal staff fairly, as well as modernise our industry and improve our service to all our customers. On strike days every effort is made by Railtrack to provide access to train operators using competent non-striking signal, supervisory and management staff. This has allowed British Rail in recent weeks to run a third of their passenger services. I hope this demonstrates our commitment to rail customers.

May I take this opportunity to offer my personal regrets to all your readers who have suffered during this unwelcome dispute.

Sincerely.

Robert Horton

P.S. Loveland-Cooper Esq
The Man at the Top
The British School of Motoring
81/87 Hartfield Road
Wimbledon
London SW19

17 February 1998

Dear Mr Loveland-Cooper

I wish to register a complaint.

Six months ago I spent a prince's ransom on a new house. I chose to move Oakleigh Road for one reason and one reason only: it is quiet. The road itself is generally devoid of through traffic and is thus particularly safe from the point of view of my two cycle-crazy children.

Unfortunately however, I have noticed that Oakleigh Road is plagued by a curious menace. The problem is that swarms of BSM marked cars spend each and every day kangarooing outside my house. Not a minute passes without a hideous "emergency stop" or a blood-curdling crunching of gears. To continue the swarm analogy, Oakleigh Road appears to akin to a honey-pot. I believe the attraction is that Oakleigh Road is on the test route.

Having been taught by BSM myself I in fact have a nostalgic sympathy for the stalling novices as they straddle the highway. That said my fellow residents and I would dearly love just a temporary respite. How about 8am to 10am on Sunday mornings?

I would be most grateful indeed if you could perform a manoeuvre of three-point-turn proportions by persuading the powers that be to practice elsewhere for just two hours a week.

I look forward to hearing from you.

Yours sincerely

Jasper Griegson

20 February 1998

81/87 Hartfield Road
London SW19 3TJ
Telephone 0181 540 8262
Fax 0181 543 7905

Dear Mr Greigson

Harrow Centre

Thank you for your fresh approach to complaining, it was much appreciated, in the nicest possible way. Your letter has been passed to me for research and reply.

Nevertheless, I fully accept that non-stop driver training would annoy even a saint and I have contacted our Harrow Centre and requested that the Manager place a notice to the effect that it would be much appreciated if instructors would distribute their training to other roads in the vicinity. I have taken the liberty of removing the name and address from your letter so that it can be read by instructors.

On a light hearted note, and meant in the best possible taste, whilst on a driving test we are no longer asked to complete a three point turn, it is now 'a turn in the road'. Without being a hazard to other road users and under control, one can manoeuvre back and forth as many times as they like - it would seem, as long as they don't hit the kerb either side. The times they are a changing!

I trust that, BSM at least, allow you the peace you so desire. Thank you for bringing the matter to our attention.

Yours sincerely

Mrs E B von Weber
Customer Relations Officerp

10

The Last Word in Complaining

I have been wrongly accused on many occasions of being a miserable, materialistic, loathsome, grumpy old git. And that just comes from my close friends and family. It has been said in particular that I spend the entirety of my existence in a cesspool of dissatisfaction.

This criticism is wholly unfounded.

For starters, I am prepared to give credit where credit is due. On 31st August 1987 I wrote a letter of compliment to the AA. I received a charming reply but the experience of mutual admiration left me with a slightly sickly taste in my mouth. At least in the middle of a bloody confrontation you know where you stand. I have not written such a letter since to the AA or anyone else. I will only do so again when (to quote the wording on the side of Cadbury's chocolate bar wrappers) I am *entirely satisfied*.

My other reason for rejecting the condemnation of those who don't like me is that they simply don't understand me. They do not realise that I am trying to elevate complaining out of the moral doldrums into a concept very close to a spiritual experience. Perhaps one day this book will be seen as a brilliant rival to the Bible, the Koran and the complete works of Mao, all rolled into one. Or am

I getting ahead of myself?

In any event, one person who does appreciate the spiritual content of my wisdom is the Pope. Last year my family and I suffered the emotional trauma of moving house. Shortly before the exchange of contracts we were told that the purchase, and indeed the entire chain, might collapse due to a 'technical hitch'. The hitch was that the Catholic Church had never given its consent to the erection of the house which we wanted to buy. In the absence of such consent, the title to the property was defective. Practising what I preach I took the only course open to me when the Catholic Church's administration failed to come up with the goods. I faxed the Pope. To be precise sent an E-mail message to the papal website. Although His Holiness did not come to the rescue, Cardinal Hume's assistant did help and the problem sorted itself out. This episode in my life has left me with a conundrum which I have yet to resolve: who would I have written to if the problem had not been solved and what is His fax number?

Please send your answers on a postcard to anyone but me.

The Customer Relations Manager
The Automobile Association
Stanmore
Middlesex

31st August 1987

Dear Sir

I write further to the assistance given to me yesterday
by one of your mobile mechanics. Despite the fact that
the problem was very difficult to locate your mechanic
showed exceptional patience and persistence in order to
get me back on the road. I would be most grateful if
you would ensure that he is properly praised for what
was an excellent job and well worthy of the standards I
have come to expect from your organization.

Yours faithfully

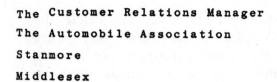

Jasper Griegson

The Automobile Association

Fanum House, The Broadway, Stanmore, Middx., HA7 4DF,
Tel: 01 954 7373 ext. 4999
Director General O. F. LAMBERT CBE

Please quote our reference:

GJM/SMM/918

11th September 1987

Dear Mr Griegson

Thank you for your letter of the 31st August and I was pleased to learn that our Patrol provided you with such good service.

I will ensure that the Patrol is advised of your very kind comments and I do appreciate the time and trouble you have taken in writing on this subject.

Yours sincerely,

G. J. MEADOWS,
Regional Manager,
Road Services - London.